COFFEE FOR ONE

COFFEE FOR ONE

How the New Way to Make Your Morning
Brew Became a Tempest in a Coffee Pod

KJ Fallon

Skyhorse Publishing

Skyhorse Publishing books may be purchased in bulk at special discounts for sales promotion, corporate gifts, fund-raising, or educational purposes. Special editions can also be created to specifications. For details, contact the Special Sales Department, Skyhorse Publishing, 307 West 36th Street, 11th Floor, New York, NY 10018 or info@skyhorsepublishing.com.

Skyhorse® and Skyhorse Publishing® are registered trademarks of Skyhorse Publishing, Inc.®, a Delaware corporation.

Visit our website at www.skyhorsepublishing.com.

10 9 8 7 6 5 4 3 2 1

Library of Congress Cataloging-in-Publication Data is available on file.

Cover design by Rain Saukas

Print ISBN: 978-1-5107-2554-6
Ebook ISBN: 978-1-5107-2555-3

Printed in the United States of America

This book is dedicated to my family because,
in the end, that is what matters

Without my morning coffee I'm just like a dried up piece of roast goat.

—Johann Sebastian Bach

Contents

Preface ix
Introduction xiii

PART ONE
FROM CROP TO CUP THROUGH THE DECADES 1

CHAPTER 1—Coffee Consumption; from Flat to Flat White. 3
CHAPTER 2—A Sixty-Second Take on the Sometimes-Subversive
Journey of Coffee through History 21
CHAPTER 3—The Journey from Tree to Table. 29

PART TWO
LOVING THE SINGLE LIFE? 33

CHAPTER 4—Rise of the Single Serve. 35
CHAPTER 5—The K-Cup, an Industry Standard 47
CHAPTER 6—The Nascent Keurig and the K-Cup 59
CHAPTER 7—K-Cup, Etcetera. 71
CHAPTER 8—Turf Wars: Keep Your Pod Out of My Brewer. 79

PART THREE
COFFEE FOR ONE EVOLVES 85

CHAPTER 9—The Single-Serve Environmental Quandary
and Some Alternatives. 87
CHAPTER 10—Giving Back 97
CHAPTER 11—Coffee and Health. 103

CHAPTER 12—Does Single Serve Fuel Too Much Separateness?.....115
CHAPTER 13—Just What is Single Serve Anyway? 121
CHAPTER 14—What's Next for Coffee for One?................129

Acknowledgments 135
Endnotes...137
Bibliography...153

Preface

Coffee is so ubiquitous in our culture that when a die-hard tea drinker I know went into a deli and ordered "Tea to go," the guy behind the counter handed my friend two containers of coffee with lids.

Every year, more than 500 billion cups of coffee are served. Coffee fuels our existence. It is our push in the morning and the afternoon. Much has been written about the origins of coffee as a beverage and even the romance of coffee, using this brewing method or that one to bring out the true essence of whatever bean and whatever roast you have chosen to be transformed into a delicious, aromatic elixir. But let's face it. Most of the time, we want to have what we want and need as quickly as possible. This is where the near instant gratification of the single-serve coffee option comes in.

About 100 million people groggily reach for a cup of coffee first thing in the morning, and the single-serve brewing method is the fastest way to get that cup of java into their hands. Coffee wakes us up, keeps us up, and even provides health benefits, including burning fat and decreasing the risk of type 2 diabetes and the most common type of liver cancer, according to recent studies. Clearly, the beverage from the bean is a major part of life, and 54 percent of Americans over the age of eighteen are coffee drinkers.

A lot of folks have pushed the usual methods of making coffee—the percolator, the French press, and even Mr. Coffee-type brewers—off into the appliance nostalgia closet. Oh, sure, coffee connoisseurs will display and even use their French press or siphon or vacuum pots. And people still brew coffee using any manner of common and esoteric methods—cold brewing, vacuum pot, AeroPress. And we all like a little variety. But as a basic and everyday way to make a cup of coffee, the single-serve brewer is here to stay and has found a permanent place on the kitchen counter. This is one small appliance that is not going to go away. It will evolve, but it will not disappear. Uses for it and variations of it will continue to develop. For instance, CVS pharmacy offers cold medicine in a single-serve cup meant to be dispensed via a single cup compatible brewer. Single serve is a singular phenomenon that will continue to grow and become more ingrained in our culinary culture.

Consumers now think nothing about spending the equivalent of more than fifty dollars a pound for ordinary coffee in single-serve pods or cups. Single-serve coffee says as much about our lifestyles as it does about how we make our coffee. Single serve is practically the only coffee brewing method an entire generation knows. This is what they grew up with and how they measure their coffee needs. Single-serve coffee has become so ingrained in our lives that the National Coffee Association USA (NCA), which, since 1950, has commissioned an annual survey about coffee consumption in the United States, recently broke out single serve into a separate category for market and trends research. In 2013, about fifteen billion single-serve coffee capsules were sold worldwide.

Many coffee lovers cannot remember a time when the machine that brewed and dispensed coffee one convenient cup at time did not exist. According to a National Coffee Association study, "since 2012 single-cup brewers have been the second most used coffee preparation method." And the percentage of coffee drinkers who had coffee brewed in a single-serve brewer the previous day is on the rise.[1]

It is as much about the pods as it is about the brewer, perhaps even more so. Keeping consumers hooked on a particular brand of pod or cup is the money maker. And drink lots of coffee, they do. The 2017 National Coffee Drinking Trends survey found that: "In 2017, a total of 33% of households claim to own this type of brewer. This compares to 29% in 2016. We also see increased interest versus 2016 in buying a single-cup brewer in the next six months. This argues for continued growth of the systems."[2]

As a lifelong coffee lover (who also appreciates a myriad variety of teas), it is my hope that the coffee-loving reader will enjoy learning about the evolution of single-serve coffee, and the failures, fights, and fiascos that have littered the road to best in cup.

The single serve represents not just a brewing sea change for the US forty billion-dollar coffee industry, but a lifestyle shift. No need for a pot of coffee for a family or group. At the office, no one has to be responsible for making a fresh pot of coffee. You can make fresh-brewed coffee just for yourself, using one hand, in under a minute.

The story of specialty coffee and single serve includes Green Day, Hugh Jackman, George Clooney, and a host of others who recognize the place that coffee has in our world.

Introduction

While this book started out as a long look at single-serve coffee and how it has become a part of life, it turned out to involve so much more. What was it about coffee culture that led to the single-serve option in the first place? Single-serve coffee did not appear in a vacuum. It took many years to get to the point where coffee lovers expected to be able to brew a fresh cup of coffee pretty much wherever and whenever they wanted. Imagine if a single-serve brewer had appeared somehow in, say, 1955, like in *Back to the Future*. I suspect that the people in the McFly household during that time period would have seen no use for such a gadget. "Make just one cup of coffee for just one person? Why? What about the rest of us who want some coffee? I have a whole can of coffee right here. Opened it two weeks ago and there's still lots left."

Well, it is all about what you're used to, right?

Specialty coffee is the breakout spin-off from what past generations of coffee lovers had previously thought of as coffee. And specialty coffee has become ever more specialized. Is your specialty coffee shop not specialized enough for you? How about an even more specialized coffee bar inside the specialty coffee shop? Starbucks did just that when it opened Starbucks Reserve Bars in some of their stores. Starbucks also has specialized Roasteries where their premium, small-lot Reserve coffee beans are roasted. The Roasteries also serve the premium coffees. Starbucks has even announced it was opening a Roastery in Milan, Italy, in late 2018. Italy, where, according to *Italy* magazine:

"It would be fair to say that Italians are passionate about coffee. So much so, you would think they had discovered it. They didn't. To make up for this, however, they have invented a coffee culture unequalled anywhere else in the world."[1]

PART ONE

FROM CROP TO CUP
THROUGH THE DECADES

CHAPTER I

Coffee Consumption; from Flat to Flat White

Coffee is usually the first sip of the morning. It is the beverage that opens the eyes to a new day and prepares our nervous system for whatever the forces throw our way. Brewing coffee in coffee pots from humble metal to decorative ceramic has been around for a very long time. Over the years this basic design evolved into the percolator and electric percolator, which worked fine for a family or group having their coffee at the same time. Other methods were also embraced by those who had the time and the inclination to go gourmet. The elegant but slow French press, the very leisurely drip method, the unhurried pour over. The sometimes near theatrical preparation was an integral part of the process. Whatever the choice, a special grind of coffee was needed for each different brewing technique. In any case, preparing the coffee was going to take time. No quick fix there. Preparing the morning brew using these low-concept methods would take a big chunk out of the morning.

What was behind the desire for a fresh-brewed single serve? When did coffee drinkers realize that they could hope for, and get, great-tasting coffee one cup at a time, really fast? Sure, there was instant, and the quality of that seemed to be improving, but would it ever be possible to have a quick fresh-brewed cup of coffee before heading out the door in the morning?

You're Drinking What with Breakfast?

Coffee wasn't always in the spotlight on the beverage stage. Coffee consumption in the Unites States peaked around 1945, with folks drinking about forty-six gallons per person.

But another beverage was starting to become a lot more popular starting at around that time. (No, not beer. Beer, along with ale, was the popular drink for breakfast or anytime in the eighteenth century.[1]) Soda. The real beverage love of people's lives was soda.

While consumption of coffee had been flat for years, after 1962 there was a marked decline in coffee drinking. In 1962, about 75 percent of adults in the United States drank coffee. By 1988, just 50 percent were coffee drinkers. Not only were there fewer coffee drinkers, those coffee drinkers were drinking fewer cups of coffee. In 1962, coffee drinkers were quaffing around three cups a day. By 1980, the amount of coffee being imbibed per day was slightly more than two cups and by 1991, that amount fell to less than two cups per day. And the people who were drinking the coffee were those in an older generation. Where were the people in their twenties? An older population with little interest in coffee drinking and a younger generation that didn't care so much for coffee didn't bode well for the longevity of coffee as a permanent part of the food and beverage habits of consumers. What were the younger people drinking? Yes. Soda. As coffee consumption fell, soda consumption rose, and at a very bubbly and steady pace.[2]

Coffee was getting seriously displaced by the cold, carbonated way to get caffeine, even in the morning. It was faster, it was more convenient, and it was just a lot . . . more . . . cool. At least that's what the soda makers wanted folks to take away from their "Coke in the Morning" ad campaign back in the 1980s and more recently with a variation on that theme. Having your morning caffeine via a refreshing, cold, and easy-to-carry soda was very appealing to a lot of consumers. They didn't have to wait in line to fill a flimsy Styrofoam cup with what was likely over-brewed coffee in the convenience store, and, if they were having breakfast at home, they didn't have to bother with measuring the coffee and waiting around while it brewed, and waiting some more while it cooled enough to drink. Why not just open the refrigerator and grab a soda with a decent amount of caffeine and bring along another one for the road? Or two.

Add to that Pepsi's "Pepsi A.M." campaign. Pepsi A.M. had 28 percent more caffeine than regular Pepsi but still about 75 percent less than the amount of caffeine in coffee. Then, sometime in the 1990s a few test markets got the chance to try Pepsi Kona and Pepsi Cappuccino.[3, 4]

Not enough? Then, how about Coca-Cola BlāK, a coffee-flavored cola? This coffee-ish soda was available for a short time in 2006. Coca-Cola likely was trying to interest the gourmet coffee lover with this very seductive-looking beverage bottle and its advertising campaign. After about two years the product was discontinued.[5] Another coffee and soda combination was Café-Cola, produced in the 1990s. (Cafe Cola 2017)[6]

It is evident that while soda was king, coffee was still an influence that soft drink manufacturers wanted to exploit. And for a lot of people, a cold caffeinated beverage with maybe a caffeine infusion was just what they wanted. They would rather have a cold soda than a cup of probably not-so-fresh-coffee. Plus, maybe they just didn't like the taste of coffee. Maybe this was because the coffee they were exposed to was just bad coffee. And there was that time thing, again. Who had time to wait around for a pot of coffee to brew? Why not just have an ice-cold Coke? If you needed more caffeine, just have another, and maybe another. Plus, for a lot of workers on fluctuating work schedules, the first meal of the day often just went better with a cold soda.

In 1985, Jolt Cola promised all of the sugar and twice the caffeine.[7] (There is a Facebook page dedicated to bringing it back.)[8] All you had to do was open the refrigerator, grab it, drink it, and go. Or drink it on the go. This was a lot less cumbersome than making coffee in the morning, especially considering that probably half the pot would be poured down the drain anyway since there was so little time to drink more than one hastily prepared cup. Soda consumption was going up, while coffee consumption was going down. You can be sure that coffee organizations took notice.

Of course, there was instant coffee, but even with that you had to wait for the water to boil and then stir it and wait some more for the coffee to cool down so you could drink it. And then if you wanted a second cup, you'd have to do it all over again.

So, enticing people to come back to or to start drinking coffee in the morning, never mind at other times, was going to take some effort, imagination, and forethought. Consumers would have to start being persuaded that, hey, maybe they should rethink their love affair with soda, which was ongoing for generations.

Part of the pullback to coffee was due to a gradual evolution on the one hand, but also to a few more revolutionary events. And they all seemed to have happened around the same time.

Revolution #1: Mr. Coffee (1972)

Its name is now synonymous with electric drip coffeemakers, but back in 1972 when it was first introduced for home use, Mr. Coffee was a brand-new idea in the world of making fresh coffee at home. Here was a machine that in one compartment you just had to fill with water and in another compartment place a filter laden with ground coffee, plug it in, turn it on, and wait, but with a wait that was a lot shorter than with other brewing methods. Plus, you didn't have to watch over it to make sure it didn't boil over or burn. It was all automatic. You could get on with whatever else you needed to do and the coffee would practically make itself.

Mr. Coffee was a resounding success, selling more than a million units in two years and was hailed as a revolutionary food preparation device.[9] And it was.

Revolution #2: The Birth of Coffeehouse Culture in the United States

McNulty's—1895

This establishment goes back a long time before specialty coffee became a phenomenon. Since the early twentieth century, this landmark for coffee and tea lovers has been offering the best of coffees and teas in Manhattan's West Village. True, there is only the one store (the store first opened not far from its current location)—but *what* a coffee (and tea) emporium, singular in every respect. Here, coffee lovers have come to know the best coffee available and have come to expect nothing less. Folks outside the New York area can order online, and McNulty's continues to get a high ranking and not just due to nostalgia. It is a favorite with tourists, as well. A step inside reveals the heady smells of so many gourmet coffees—it is hard to choose the one or ones you want to try.

McNulty's has been around for a very long time and may be in just one small location, but they are further proof that people will seek out fine coffees once they are awakened to the pleasures this perfect beverage offers. These coffee lovers learned that settling for mediocre coffee is not an option.

There really cannot be too many gourmet coffeehouses. Even though other coffee emporiums have opened nearby it only enhances what McNulty's has to offer. There is no such thing, it seems, as too many choices of where to find the perfect cup of coffee.

Peet's Coffee

Peet's Coffee is the brainchild of Holland-born Alfred Peet, who knew pretty much everything there was to know about coffee. He came to the United States after World War II and was flabbergasted at the swill that Americans referred to as coffee. Seeing it as his mission to set things right, he opened his first store in 1966 in Berkeley, California. His method was a forerunner of the gourmet preparation of coffee. He prepared his coffee in small batches using fresh beans that were dark roasted. The result was a cup of coffee that opened the eyes, taste buds, and souls of coffee drinkers. So *this* is what coffee was supposed to taste like!

Three years later, Peet's Coffee & Tea was renowned as a popular place for coffee lovers to gather. The area became known as the Gourmet Ghetto where coffee lovers and foodies (although the term didn't exist at the time) could meet up and take it all in, in the form of rich, deep coffee, exciting new foods, and stimulating conversation. This was a new era for coffee entrepreneurs.

Peet's coffee devotees were known as "Peetniks." Today there are close to 250 Peet's stores in seven states and Washington, DC, and Peet's is now part of JAB Holdings (more about JAB later).

Starbucks

Founded on the idea that people wanted great coffee, Starbucks began as a single store in the historic district of Pike's Place in Seattle, Washington, in 1971 and has grown into many different things to many different people. They were at the forefront of getting consumers interested in, and educated about, really good coffee. The seeds for expansion from a single store to a worldwide phenomenon began in 1982 when Howard Schultz came onboard. Later, a trip to espresso bars in the Italian city of Piazza del Duomo—seeing firsthand the serious coffee culture with animated patrons relaxing and conversing—convinced Schultz that the coffeehouse ethos could be done and would do well in the United States.[10] (And now Howard Schultz is taking the idea back to Italy with those Starbucks Roasteries.)

Over the years, Starbucks has offered beverages of varying sophistication and uniqueness, and customers have been eager to try not only delicious, gourmet coffees, but also to explore the different variations on the coffee theme that Starbucks offered. So, with the growing popularity and availability of the fine coffees that Starbucks served, an increasing number of coffee drinkers and coffee converts were becoming aware that the coffee that they drank didn't have to be predictable or dull. Coffee held many possibilities for an adventure in caffeine imbibing.

Now with more than twenty-two thousand stores worldwide and more than thirty blends and premium single-origin coffees, Starbucks is firmly entrenched as a part of the coffee culture.

Revolution #3: The Coffee Bag—Making One Cup of Coffee at a Time

This might be a bit of a stretch, but think about it. It was in the 1980s that coffee drinkers started to wake up to the idea that they could have a cup of fresh-brewed—not a variation of instant—coffee and get on with their day faster. Now, this is more about being able to make a single cup of coffee at home. It would not be of the same quality as the coffee served in gourmet coffeehouse, but it would be fresher tasting than instant coffee. When opening a box of single-serve coffee bags, such as Maxwell House Singles, you would be met with the agreeable scent of fresh-enough coffee.

Folgers and Maxwell House introduced coffee singles, which were like oversized tea bags filled with coffee that, when placed in a cup with hot water, would steep and brew into a cup of coffee. This method followed the principle of the tea bag, and the coffee brewed fairly quickly right in the mug, but something was missing. While you could, in theory, brew your coffee in a cup á la tea bag, some thought there remained a bit of an aftertaste. It was coffee. It was pretty fast. And it was fresh brewed. But it wasn't . . . great.

Coffee singles are still readily available and are convenient, for sure. There is a variation on this, a paper-filter-placed-over-a-cup method known as Japanese Pour Over Coffee, which is more of a drip method not unlike the cone filter pour-over that can be used with a pot or a single cup.

Cone filters produced by companies like Melitta offered the option of making drip coffee one cup at a time, but this was not always convenient and it did not save much time. If you needed to get going and out of the house, standing around waiting for the beverage to drip through the filter into your mug or cup took too long. If you had the wrong type of coffee grinds, the cone filter paper would either get clogged or the liquid that filtered down into your cup became too weak. And unless you were using a clear mug so you could see what was going on, the coffee could overflow onto the counter.

One thing is clear: once the option for making one cup at a time started to appear, the thirst for a better cup-at-a-time grew. And the need for continuously improving the results naturally followed. Coffee drinkers were starting to really like the idea of having their morning java fast *and* fresh brewed.

But there was something else stirring, seemingly unrelated to gourmet coffee. You might not think that the economy could be a driving force behind the rise of the popularity of gourmet coffee, but it was. The late 1970s and the beginning of the 1980s saw rising interest rates and inflation, and with that brought a shift in how coffee was traded and the size of inventories ordered.

A paper by the late anthropologist William Roseberry, "The Rise of Yuppie Coffees and the Reimagination of Class in the United States," very effectively captures how coffee was affected by attitudes, marketing, and consumption, and how, in turn, coffee attitudes, marketing, and consumption over a period of about twenty years affected consumer behavior.

About forty years ago, by Roseberry's account, selling coffee was all about the price. The cheaper, the better. Procter & Gamble and General Foods were behind most of the popular brands. Most people bought their coffee in cans in a supermarket. They had a brand that they liked and went with that. End of story.[11]

The turn to more specialized coffee—gourmet coffee—is, in some ways, a return to an even more distant past, when coffee beans were bought in smaller batches and small emporiums prepared the beans to their customers' satisfaction.

The consumption of coffee was steadily declining. Brazil was, and still is, the world's largest coffee producer. A very severe frost in July 1975 in Brazil wiped out two-thirds of their coffee crop and caused coffee prices to increase fivefold, and was widely reported in the news.[12] Wholesalers and consumers felt the pain, and coffee drinkers launched boycotts to protest the extraordinary price hikes. Thus, coffee purchases dropped precipitously. The 1975 damaging frost was followed in 1981 by another that was not as severe but still, between 15 and 50 percent of Brazil's coffee crop was damaged.[13, 14, 15]

Things were not looking so great for coffee at the start of the 1980s. But something else was beginning to percolate around that time. While the consumption of coffee in general declined, a relatively new niche market started to arise from the burnt grounds of the old way people thought about coffee—the specialty coffee market.

The Rise of Specialty Coffee

It would take an advertising executive to see where the coffee industry was going wrong, and looking back, it seems so obvious. Why did no one see this before? Kenneth Roman Jr. was the head of Ogilvy & Mather, one of the top advertising firms in New York City. Ogilvy & Mather happened to have Maxwell House as a client. Roseberry reports that in an interview with *World Coffee and Tea*, Roman detailed an interesting reason for the problems the coffee industry was having. He also, very helpfully, outlined some solutions.[16]

Roman had the brilliant observation that for much too long coffee had been marketed purely on price. What was the lowest price that coffee could command? Everyone was missing a major point. Why was coffee being marketed in terms of how much it cost? Like a true advertising professional, Roman said that coffee should be marketed based on its value, image, and quality. Roman understood that selling for price alone, on how low can the price go, was a lose-lose situation. How about, he asked, selling coffee on its taste, its smell, and its appearance, instead?[17]

Roman also astutely observed that that time period was the cusp of the "Me Generation." Consumers wanted to know how coffee related to them and how coffee fit with their lifestyle, and so on. The coffee company that could answer those questions satisfactorily was the coffee company that would win the hearts and minds of consumers.[18]

Roman also took things a step further, as Roseberry explained. In 1981, speaking to the Green Coffee Association, a coffee trade organization, Roman emphasized the need to think of the coffee as a product not for the mass market but for a segmented market. He thought that it made more sense to think of the market in terms of generation and class. Roman thought that college students who were not yet coffee drinkers, as well as yuppies, should be the primary focus of specialty coffees. It would be more successful to target the yuppie couple with fine varietal coffees and aim at reaching college students through flavored coffees, which might help wean them off soda.[19]

Diversification and not standardization was what would work to get coffee out there in the future. That was very different from the perspective the coffee industry had been operating from for quite some time. It was obvious that things had to change. Trying to sell coffee to the multitudes as a product for mass consumption was not working anymore. Society was changing and the marketing of coffee had to change with it.

Roseberry muses that it was odd that coffee was ever marketed in a standardized way. Coffee just by its nature is a perfect fit for segmented marketing since coffee itself is a diverse product.

Coffee is a lot more than just a drink; it's something happening. Not as in hip, but like an event, a place to be, but not like a location, but like somewhere within yourself. It gives you time, but not actual hours or minutes, but a chance to be, like be yourself, and have a second cup.
—Gertrude Stein

The time was right for the emergence of the specialty coffee sector. Coffee and coffee drinking were not only becoming culturally hip, they were also becoming a very smart and forward-thinking business move. An increasing number of gourmet coffee and specialty food shops popped up around the country. Who wanted to pay for boring, nondescript coffee when you could find a stellar gourmet brew down the block?

By their nature, the appeal of these small shops was that they offered thoughtfully chosen coffees in small batches. Coffee, on the other hand, was imported, stored, and sold in mass quantities. How would this work if the buyers of the specialty shops made their livelihood by purchasing a range of coffees in smaller quantities?

Enter the roaster. As Roseberry observed, the roaster was becoming more important to the smaller specialty coffee shops.

There were already smaller roasters around the country who supplied some restaurants, shops, and other locations. The roaster deals with the importer of the coffee beans, choosing the types of coffee and the quantities that his or her clients—the small specialty shops—would want to buy. Green coffee beans can be stored for quite a long time. It is only once the beans are roasted that the countdown away from freshness begins. The roaster can buy exactly the selection that the smaller shops require for their customers and roast as little as a few pounds at a time.

Since coffee deteriorates quickly after it is roasted, location of the roaster is everything. So more roasters meant more coffee shops in the area of the roasters and vice versa. Seattle and the San Francisco Bay area on the West Coast were some of the early hotbeds of these specialty coffee shops and their roasters. Sometimes a large roaster would set up a specialty roasting option to better serve the clients who wanted coffee in small and specialized batches. Known as regional roasters, they soon became an integral part of the expanding specialty coffee business at the retail level. It was the roasters who developed new roasts, different blends, and held sessions to better educate the retailers about the coffee they were selling. Everyone learned more about specialty coffee and everyone benefited because the result was truly the best cup of coffee possible.[20]

But there were some snags for the roasters when it came to procuring the coffee. The big importers and warehouse managers were not keen on breaking their huge quantities of coffee beans into smaller-sized bags.

The specialty coffee network of roaster and retailer was still pretty small in the 1980s. The New York City area was not as quick to embrace the tentative moves to a smaller and more specialized coffee market as was the West Coast. But the NYC area specialty coffee market was growing. In the latter part of the 1980s, the demand for specialty coffee that was roasted in small batches was greater than what could be supplied, especially in the New York area.

So the network of roasters and retail establishments that specialized in gourmet coffees had to be very tight, geographically speaking. Since once the beans were roasted they would start to lose their freshness, they had to get to the retail establishment from the roaster quickly.

Then came a little improvement known as valve packaging. You know those little hard round disc-shaped things on bags of ground and whole bean coffee? They are actually one-way degassing valves and were a pretty major breakthrough in the specialty coffee industry. The valves had been invented sometime in the late 1960s and were used in Europe, where coffee bags were widespread in the 1970s. This was a pretty important step, right up there with vacuum-packing, which began in the United States with the Hills Brothers firm packing coffee in cans in the early 1900s. The coffee can was still the choice of the big coffee conglomerates in the United States in the 1980s, but with specialty coffee growing in popularity in the United States, the bag became a preferred option and the little plastic valve ensured that the coffee inside the bag remained fresh for a lot longer.[21]

Coffee that has been freshly roasted emits lots of gas—CO_2. It's just the way it is. That gas has to go somewhere, and the valve allows the gas to safely escape from the bag. It is a one-way valve because oxygen is not good for the coffee inside of the bag. According to a producer of bags that use these valves, before these valves were invented, there were only two options for roasters—pack the coffee in paper bags that were porous and allowed the gas to escape (but then the coffee would not stay fresh for very long since the paper was permeable); or the coffee could simply degas for a certain amount of time before it was put into (usually) a can.[22]

The one-way degassing valve allowed roasters who served the smaller specialty coffee shops and gourmet outlets to widen the area to which they dispensed the product and to go even farther afield.[23]

At the same time that the specialty coffee sector was growing and more people were turning to gourmet coffee as their brew of choice, the number of people drinking coffee overall was declining. Specialty coffee was not just growing, it was booming. But, according to the research in William Roseberry's article, the large coffee distributors like General Foods, Procter & Gamble, and Nestlé figured that the specialty coffee escalation was just a fad and would not last. (Later we will see how these giants would not let another innovation escape them.)

But those that followed the coffee industry noticed, and, in 1982, the Specialty Coffee Association of America was formed. The membership-based association changed its name in 2017 to Specialty Coffee Association (SCA) after merging with the Specialty Coffee Association of Europe. The SCA represents coffee professionals worldwide, ranging from coffee farmers to roasters to baristas, and offers education, training, and other resources to those in the specialty coffee industry. The SCA works to ensure high standards for specialty coffee throughout the world.[24]

While the coffee behemoths had been skeptical about the longevity of specialty coffee, eventually they came to realize that it would make good economic sense to join the specialty coffee trend. In 1986, General Foods and A&P both brought out lines of specialty coffees to be sold in—gasp!—supermarkets. General Foods offered the Maxwell House Private Collection.[25] The ads for the Private Collection were very low-key and were aimed at the specialty coffee drinker. Television advertisement was not used, which was unusual. One print ad, for instance, featured no obvious signs that the ad was, in fact, for a kind of coffee. The magazine ad featured a man and a woman wearing white sitting in a wicker lounge chair and gazing out over inviting blue waters. The man says, "It's wonderful to get away from civilization," while the woman muses, "I wonder if I can use my credit cards." The only indication that the ad has anything to do with some kind of hot beverage were the coffee mugs the couple were holding. As an article in the *Los Angeles Times* speculated at the time, was this an ad for a clothing line or an idyllic vacation spot? Looking closer, the reader sees a small picture of a bag of coffee beans.[26] Maxwell House wanted to reach the sophisticated specialty coffee drinker and so nothing loud or obvious would do. This line, as the company advertised, featured "Private coffees for all your private moods." Maxwell House knew that the specialty coffee market had been growing over the previous four years even though the rest of the coffee market was pretty much flat. The popularity of gourmet foods in general was expanding during that time.

A&P was not going to stand by and miss getting a piece of the specialty coffee market. A&P, like General Foods, recognized that baby boomers wanted specialty coffee and other gourmet foods, and they would pay a premium price for them. Around this time A&P came out with the Royale Gourmet Bean line as a part of their Eight O'Clock Coffee line, which had been around since 1859.[27]

Both of these food conglomerates knew they needed to get serious about specialty coffee. In the meantime, though, the smaller specialty shops were not just sitting stagnant; they, too, were growing. Starbucks in Seattle was beginning to open more stores and not just in their own area. Starbucks was going national around the same time that the big coffee guys woke up to the huge market potential in specialty coffee. Things were really heating up in the gourmet coffee arena.

Another development that emerged around 1983 was flavored coffees. These consisted of adding flavors such as vanilla, cinnamon, hazelnut, etc., to freshly roasted beans. Some die-hard coffee lovers can't understand why anyone would want to add flavors to coffee. They feel that the whole point of experiencing a good cup of coffee is to enjoy the flavor of the coffee. But lots of people are in love with flavored coffees.

The idea was to entice people who had previously shunned coffee. You know, those who drank mostly soda or carbonated beverages exclusively. It may be that flavored coffees are succeeding in getting the non-coffee, carbonated beverage drinkers to come over to the coffee side, at least every so often. An alternative to spraying flavors on the fresh-roasted beans was the addition of flavored syrups to coffee drinks. Several bottles of syrups, such as those from Torani, in flavors such as almond, hazelnut, caramel, crème de cacao, and so on, exponentially increased the types of coffee concoctions a small establishment could offer its customers.

In any case, there was some skepticism whether flavored coffees would attract the soft-drink devotee. But flavored coffees, along with flavored creamers, are here to stay. For example, consumers can buy Starbucks K-Cups with natural flavors such as vanilla and caramel.

Another factor in the success and increasing customer base for specialty coffee is the ability to control certain features. For sure, there was no controlling the climate where the coffee was grown, what type of coffee the grower would be cultivating (i.e., arabica or robusta), or the place—Brazil, or Colombia, and Kona, or etc.—but roasters and specialty coffee shop owners could multiply their selections by using a bit of imagination. At the roasting and beyond stage, there were many ways to market and sell the coffee to the specialty coffee shops and, in turn, for the shops to sell to their customers. At the roasting level, the roaster might blend different beans from different areas and produce a blend that could vary from day to day.

Manés Alves is the founder of Coffee Lab International (CLI), an independent coffee testing facility in Vermont that has catered to all segments of the coffee industry since 1995—from small coffee farmers, exporters, importers, micro-roasters, and large commercial roasters, to multinational retailers, restaurant chains, cafés, and food service providers.

Manés Alves is on the Technical Standards Committee of the Specialty Coffee Association. The Technical Standards Committee is one of the longest continuously functioning volunteer committees within the SCA.

They conduct research to determine specialty coffee standards and ascertain industry best practice for publication on behalf of the Specialty Coffee Association. The SCA not only works for their members, but also the coffee industry overall.

Alves has some ideas about why specialty coffee became so very popular. One reason is that, starting in 2000, the Specialty Coffee Association started to educate the people in the industry.[28] "Up to that point, we never educated anybody," he said in an interview. "Since 2000 we came up with different programs. We, meaning the Specialty Coffee Association, that it's done through them or it's done through something like the Coffee Quality Institute, which is part of the Specialty Coffee Association." (The Coffee Quality Institute is a nonprofit organization that works on a global level to improve the quality of coffee and the lives of those who produce coffee.)

Alves said that the SCA has had programs before, since 1995 or earlier, but the programs consisted of classes that were offered once a year. The classes were about things like brewing the coffee, and were referred to as "coffee conferences." There were limited vacancies for these classes, with the largest class having maybe about 150 people. "They would fill up pretty quickly," he said, "and that would be a problem. Since then we came up with many programs, and we started to implement all these for roasting, cupping, brewing." Not only is there a barista program, there are coffee bean sales programs that provide an opportunity for people to learn very concrete issues having to do with every aspect of coffee.

In addition to what the SCA has done, a couple of universities have been showing interest in developing coffee-related programs and the resources around it. As of now, one program is specifically designed around coffee processing in Lábrea in Brazil. According to Alves, they are still in the process of launching the program, and that once ready, it will take between one and two years to complete.

Since the program has to do with harvest, those taking this course have to go to the source and do some work. "We cannot just do the program online or something like that," said Alves. "You have to go out and actually do it."

Academic institutions have started to take notice of the meteoric rise of specialty coffee, so they have started offering another way for people seriously interested in the coffee process to learn firsthand from the experts. The Coffee Center at UC Davis in California is not a place to grab a cup of coffee.[29] The Coffee Center is a place where students who want to know more about the coffee process can learn by taking part in a hands-on approach in a newly designed location that includes the Peet's Coffee Pilot Roastery, thanks to a donation in 2016 from Peet's Coffee. A couple of years prior, the university had taken notice that there was a growing interest in coffee among students—"The Design of Coffee," was voted the most popular course on campus—and started the "Coffee Initiative."

There are many learning tools for the study of coffee as a science that did not exist before. In the end, everyone with any interest in coffee benefits, from the growers to the consumer.

While the proliferation of specialty coffee was one of the factors that paved the way for the single-serve option, other events laid the groundwork for single serve.

To understand that evolution, we must take a fast walk through the coffee history chamber. A very fast walk.

CHAPTER 2

A Sixty-Second Take on the Sometimes-Subversive Journey of Coffee through History

The word coffee is like a charm. It conjures up all sorts of aromas, tastes, expectations, and memories. The heat that permeates your fingers as they embrace a warm ceramic (or porcelain or stoneware or ironstone) cup as you take that first sip. The remembrance of things caffeinated. Coffee, the beverage, emanates from coffee, the plant.

Coffee is in the family *Rubiaceae*, which also includes the species of plants or trees that give us quinine and ipecac. Coffee is known by many names to different people: café (French and Spanish), kaffee (Germans), caffe (Italians), kahvi (Finnish), koffie (Dutch), kafes (Greeks), and kaffa (Guragigna in Southwest Ethiopia, where coffee originated). There are as many legends as there is history about the journey of coffee from Ethiopia (then Abyssinia) sometime around the first century, to the mass-generated coffee in cans to specialty coffee to the single serve. According to ethiopianspecialtycoffee.com, coffea arabica has been growing wild in Africa since "time immemorial."[1]

Coffee's Provocative Path from Discovery to Obsession

The legend that is closely bound with the origins of coffee as a drink features a goat herder by the name of Kalid and takes place in the Ethiopian province of Kaffa. Kalid saw that the goats he was tending to were exceptionally energetic after eating the cherry-like fruit on some of the bushes. Kalid tried the berries as well and found them to be very stimulating. Enter a monk who came upon Kalid while in a highly energetic state. The monk decided to try the berries himself. Evidently, the monk liked how he felt because he gathered up some of the coffee cherries and planted the seeds near his monastery. Eventually, he harvested cherries from the plant and tried boiling them. The other monks drank the liquid and found that they had no trouble avoiding nodding off during the nighttime prayers.

Sometimes Misunderstood, Often Sought After, and Always Prized

Another version of this story holds that the goat herder tried the cherries when he saw that his goats were unusually lively after eating the red fruit, and he felt so euphoric that he ran home to his wife with the cherries. She suggested that her husband take them to the nearby monastery since the fruit had to be blessed in some way. The goat herder did just that and gave the cherries to the monk in charge after telling him about the wonderful powers of the berry. The head monk was not impressed. Saying that they were the work of the Devil, he threw the cherries into a fire. You can imagine what the result was. The cherries began roasting. It wasn't long before the fragrant—almost invigorating—smell of the roasting beans permeated the air. The other monks became curious and, as this version of the legend goes, the roasted beans were removed from the fireplace and broken up to thoroughly put out the cinders. Somehow, for some reason, a monk (the head monk, one must presume) dictated that the crushed beans, which now were reduced to grains, were to be placed in a large jug that was then filled with hot water. Was this the first pot of coffee? Possibly, because that night the monks drank some of the beverage and found they had no trouble staying alert throughout the night during their lengthy prayers.[2]

Still another legend says that the monks could have simply been chewing the berries for its rousing properties for centuries. For some reason, at some point, one of the monks decided to make a beverage from the fruit.

It seems there is no shortage of stories and legends when it comes to the discovery of coffee, for yet another version says that it was Sudanese slaves who chewed on the cherries, the fruits that surrounds the beans, to help them endure the journey from Ethiopia to Arabia. Coffee may also have been crushed with clarified butter and eaten like a sweet, something that is still done in Kaffa and Sidamo in Ethiopia.

Another legend says that Sheikh Omar saw some coffee plants growing uncultivated in the region of Mocha in Yemen. He picked some of the coffee cherries and placed them in boiling water, creating an invigorating beverage. This legend has many variations, including one in which Sheikh Omar presented the coffee beverage to the King of Mocha to give to his ailing daughter. Still another variation on this particular coffee theme says an enchanting bird flew to Sheikh Omar and brought him to a coffee tree laden with coffee cherries.[3]

In any case, coffee, in the initial forms it was known, was long recognized as something that benefited whoever chewed the berries or drank the beverage made from them. It stimulated the senses and sharpened the mind. If you needed to stay alert and awake, here was a solution. And it was right there growing on some bushes.

Once coffee made it to the Arabian Peninsula, the world would be next. According to the National Coffee Association USA (NCA), "By the 15th century, coffee was being grown in the Yemeni district of Arabia and by the 16th century it was known in Persia, Egypt, Syria, and Turkey."[4] Something was changing with coffee and the drinking of this lively, caffeinated beverage. People were not just having it in their house, they were gathering in coffeehouses that were open to the public. These were very social and popular places where people, in addition to drinking coffee, could take part in conversations, find out what was going on around them, and hear music. Says the NCA, "Coffee houses quickly became such an important center for the exchange of information that they were often referred to as 'Schools of the Wise.'"[5]

Coffee continued its journey East to what was then Ceylon, and by the early sixteenth century to Constantinople, where coffeehouses sprang up midcentury. Here, too, coffee was seen as a very provocative beverage and the coffeehouses were looked at with suspicion. Coffee and coffeehouses were again associated with intellectual thought and new ideas, where much debate and discussion took place. This was seen as potentially threatening and over the years both the drink and the popular establishments where coffee was consumed were banned. It was true that these gathering places could be a comfortable place where dissidents and freethinkers might associate with one another, and so their very existence might threaten the powers that be at the time, religious or secular. Even the beverage seemed to be held in either high esteem or as the source of evil: "From time to time coffee continued to be banned, the target of religious zealots, and at one time second offenders were sewn into leather bags and thrown into the Bosphorus. But coffee was profitable and finally achieved respectability when it became subject to tax."[6]

Ah yes, taxing coffee seemed to make a lot of difference in its acceptability.

By the mid-seventeenth century, coffee found its way to Europe, thanks to Venetian traders. Once again, coffee was the center of a controversy: ". . . some clerics, like the mullahs of Mecca, suggested it should be excommunicated as it was the Devil's work. However, Pope Clement VIII (1592–1605) enjoyed it so much that he declared that coffee should be baptized to make it a true Christian drink."[7]

In 1683, Venice opened its first coffeehouse, the Caffè Florian, and it is still doing business today.[8] The coming decades and century saw many coffeehouses opening throughout Europe. Here were comfortable spaces where people could gather to enjoy an enlivening cup of coffee and lively conversation. The coffeehouse concept was here to stay.

Oxford was the location of the first coffeehouse in England, which makes sense considering the educational facilities there. A couple of years later London had a coffeehouse or two, including Edward Lloyd's coffeehouse on Tower Street. Lloyd's coffeehouse was the beginning of Lloyd's of London, the 325-year-old institution that is widely known for its specialist insurance. Back in 1688, Edward Lloyd's coffeehouse was the place to go for marine insurance. London was a center for trade and there was a lot of demand for insurance for the sailing vessels that would be bringing in and taking out goods and supplies. According to Lloyd's website:

> Lloyd's was by now established at 16 Lombard Street, in the very centre of the business world, and was emerging as the location for marine underwriting by individuals. The American Revolution of the 1770s, followed by the Napoleonic Wars in the early 1800s, would soon demonstrate just how vital marine insurance could be. It would bring large profits to those who could provide it—but it also brought huge losses. During this period, Lloyd's began to dominate shipping insurance on a global scale.[9]

And it all began in a coffee shop.

According to the NCA:

> Coffee houses were quickly becoming centers of social activity and communication in the major cities of England, Austria, France, Germany and Holland. In England "penny universities" sprang up, so called because for the price of a penny one could purchase a cup of coffee and engage in stimulating conversation. Coffee began to replace the common breakfast drink beverages of the time—beer and wine. Those who drank coffee instead of alcohol began the day alert and energized, and not surprisingly, the quality of their work was greatly improved.[10]

Coffee made it to the New World, to what was then New Amsterdam, when it was settled by the Dutch. There were a good number of coffeehouses, but tea was still the favorite drink of the colonists in the New World. That is, tea was the preferred drink until King George III of England decided to levy a high tax on tea in the colonies. That tax and the revolt that followed, the Boston Tea Party, forever pushed out tea in favor of coffee as the American drink of choice. Thomas Jefferson declared coffee to be "the favorite drink of the civilized world."[11]

This is how the consuming of coffee evolved, but what about the cultivation of the coffee plant, so the beverage could be harvested in a dependable manner? Coffee growing was becoming highly prized and there was a lot of competition among coffee plantations. Convenient for the countries in Europe, they had quite a few colonies that offered a suitable climate for growing *Coffea arabica*. The Dutch, for example, had Sri Lanka and Surinam. Coffee was then planted in South America, the future hub for coffee growing, and Africa in British East Africa (Kenya), in the late nineteenth century, not far from where it all began in Ethiopia, which is a very big coffee bean exporter today.

In 1714, Amsterdam's mayor gave French King Louis XIV a fledgling coffee plant, which the king had planted in Paris's Royal Botanical Garden, according to the NCA. Almost ten years later a naval officer, Gabriel de Clieu, procured a cutting from the royal coffee plant: "Despite a challenging voyage—complete with horrendous weather, a saboteur who tried to destroy the seedling, and a pirate attack—he managed to transport it safely to Martinique. Once planted, the seedling not only thrived, but it's credited with the spread of over 18 million coffee trees on the island of Martinique in the next 50 years. Even more incredible is that this seedling was the parent of all coffee trees throughout the Caribbean, South and Central America."[12]

Seduction may have played a part in how coffee found its way to Brazil. There are different versions of the story (of course) but the gist is that Francisco de Mello Palheta, an officer who was sent to Cayenne, French Guiana, to settle some sort of political or land dispute (or he was sent there to get coffee plant seedlings) ended up absconding with coffee plants, even though they were heavily guarded. But the armaments of the guards were no match for his charm. The governor's wife, entranced by his charisma, gave Francisco a bouquet in which coffee plant seeds had been carefully hidden. From these seeds grew the coffee industry that makes Brazil undisputedly the largest coffee producing country in the world.[13] By the way, the second largest coffee-producing country? Vietnam.[14]

Over the following decades, coffee seeds were dispersed through the travels of traders, missionaries, and others who regularly went from one land to another. As the NCA says, "Plantations were established in magnificent tropical forests and on rugged mountain highlands. Some crops flourished, while others were short-lived. New nations were established on coffee economies. Fortunes were made and lost. By the end of the 18th century, coffee had become one of the world's most profitable export crops. After crude oil, coffee is the most sought commodity in the world."[15]

There you have a very abbreviated version of how coffee found its way around the world. But, what about how it gets from where it grows to your mug?

CHAPTER 3

The Journey from Tree to Table

While coffee's journey from where it is grown to the coffee drinker's cup may not be as perilous or fraught with danger as the journey centuries ago from its discovery to worldwide enjoyment, there are still many steps from coffee tree to your brewer. Ten steps, to be exact, according to the National Coffee Association USA (NCA).[1]

Everything starts, as it so often does, with a seed. Coffee beans are the seeds of the coffee plant. These are the same beans that are dried, roasted, and ground to make the perfect brew of coffee. Without all of this processing, the bean stays a seed that can be planted to grow more coffee plants. Young coffee plants need just the right amount of sun, shade, moisture, and fertilizer to produce an abundant crop.

After at least three years, the coffee plants produce fruit, the coffee cherry. When it is ready to be picked, it turns a bright red. The plants usually yield one harvest a year, but there can be a second harvest in some countries, like Colombia, for instance. The arduous task of picking the coffee cherries comes next. Usually the coffee is harvested by hand, which is a very painstaking process. In places where the terrain is more level, machinery can be used to harvest the fruit.

There are two ways to gather the coffee: strip picking—where each and every cherry is picked from the tree—or selective picking—where only the cherries that are ripe are picked; this is done by hand. This method is used mostly for the arabica beans, which are descended from the original Ethiopian coffee plants and bring high prices in the marketplace.[2] According to the NCA, "A good picker averages approximately 100 to 200 pounds of coffee cherries a day, which will produce 20 to 40 pounds of coffee beans. Each worker's daily haul is carefully weighed, and each picker is paid on the merit of his or her work."[3]

The third step in the coffee plant-to-cup method is processing. This has to be done fast so the fruit doesn't spoil. There are two ways to process the coffee cherries: the dry method and the wet method. With the dry method, which is useful in places where water is scarce, the coffee fruit is strewn about on immense surfaces to be sun dried. The fruit must be covered from the rain and during the night to protect it. This method can take weeks.

With the wet method, a pulping machine removes the pulp and skin from the beans; then the beans travel through troughs of water, and the heavy, ripe beans go to the bottom while the beans that are not quite ripe drift upward. After passing through spinning drums, the beans are deposited into fermentation tanks that further slough off more layers of material clinging to the beans.[4]

The fourth step is drying the beans (if the wet processing method has been used). The beans can be dried by the warmth of the sun or with a tumble dryer. At this point the dried beans are referred to as parchment coffee.

The fifth step is milling. As the NCA says, "hulling machinery removes the parchment layer (endocarp) from wet processed coffee. Hulling dry processed coffee refers to removing the entire dried husk—the exocarp, mesocarp, and endocarp—of the dried cherries."[5]

An elective step in the milling process involves polishing the beans. After the beans have been hulled, any silver skin still on the beans is removed. While polished beans are thought to be of a better quality than unpolished beans, there really is hardly any difference between the two. Next comes grading and sorting. This involves sorting by weight, size, and imperfections in color and such.

Then comes the exporting of the beans, which at this point are called green coffee. The green coffee is put into sisal or jute bags and shipped.[6]

The next step is tasting, which doesn't refer to sipping a cup of coffee that has been brewed at home or in a coffee shop—this is something entirely different. This tasting is called *cupping*, a way to accurately assess the quality of the coffee. As the Specialty Coffee Association (SCA) explains, there is a strict protocol to cupping.[7]

The cupper visually inspects the beans. Some beans are then roasted in a small roaster, ground right away, and put into boiling water. The aroma of this little brew is very important. The cupper tastes the mixture after checking the aroma again—there is a special way the coffee is tasted. This is a very involved and very important process and requires a well-trained cupper. Says the NCA: "Coffees are not only analyzed to determine their characteristics and flaws, but also for the purpose of blending different beans or creating the proper roast. An expert cupper can taste hundreds of samples of coffee a day and still taste the subtle differences between them."[8]

Roasting, the process by which the green beans become the heady and fragrant coffee beans we all know and love, comes next. The beans are kept constantly moving in an oven that is 550 degrees Fahrenheit. Not long after, the oily and aromatic caffeol comes out of the beans.

Grinding the beans comes next, and how fine or coarse the grind is depends on the brewing method: "The length of time the grounds will be in contact with water determines the ideal grade of grind. Generally, the finer the grind, the more quickly the coffee should be prepared. That's why coffee ground for an espresso machine is much finer than coffee brewed in a drip system. Espresso machines use 132 pounds per square inch of pressure to extract coffee."[9]

Lastly, comes the brewing, and everyone is familiar with this.

Manés Alves's Coffee Lab International works with clients and their roasting partners as an independent Quality Assurance lab, which is crucial, according to their website: "Underlying coffee quality problems can be complex; from the integrity of the green beans, improper storage, and inconsistencies between roasts; to packaging deficiencies, blends that are out of spec, equipment issues, and lack of proper staff training."[10]

Things can go wrong during any one of the steps, including things that can affect the taste of the coffee at the end of its journey. The different steps have to be done at the right times, starting with the planting.

The coffee that is planted, of course, has to be adapted to the area where it is going to grow. Some plants are, to a certain extent, more hardy and pest resistant, but they are often not the best for cupping. While they are good in terms of yield, they are not so good in terms of quality.

"After you pick the coffee, the quality is there," Alves said. "There's nothing else you can do to improve it . . . The only thing you can do is actually destroy it. Destroy the quality that is already there. It's actually much easier to destroy the quality than preserve the quality."

At the hulling stage the quality can be maintained or lost. Same with storage and with the journey from where it was produced to where it is being shipped. "Let's say your coffee comes from Kenya," Alves explained. "If you don't have the coffee inside a plastic container, by the time it gets here it's going to be at least four points lower. Imagine you score the coffee at ninety. By the time the coffee gets here it's going to be an eighty-six."[11]

Roasting is another stage where missteps can happen and affect the coffee quality. Roasting slipups are, according to Alves, a huge problem. This usually happens more frequently with small roasters that do not have the tools to figure out how to be consistent from roast to roast. Alves said that there are different color meters that can be used to show what color has been achieved when the coffee is roasted. Twenty or so years ago the least expensive of these tools would cost $20,000. Now they are available for around $2,000 and do the same thing.

Blends can also be out of spec. And what is that? A blend out of spec means that a certain type of blend has been set up with a certain type of flavor profile. If, when the coffee is tasted, the tasters find that the blend does not hit all the different points that it is supposed to hit, the blend is out of spec.

So concludes a very condensed version of the journey of coffee from where it is planted and grown to your cup. Now, about that single serve . . .

PART TWO

LOVING THE SINGLE LIFE?

CHAPTER 4
Rise of the Single Serve

Coffee consumption awareness led to specialty coffee, which eventually led to brewing coffee by the cup. A product came on the scene that had a tremendous impact on the success of single-serve coffee. It was a very compact and portable coffee brewer by Salton. Salton was known for their yogurt maker that could make yogurt overnight; it was very successful. Salton is also known for marketing the George Foreman Grill, which promised to grill in a healthier way right at home. In 2003, Salton came out with a small, compact coffee brewer that brewed one cup at a time, using a soft coffee pod.

This came about when Salton discovered there was a factory in China that had been making brewers for another company. That company had to move the enterprise to a location better suited to their needs.[1] That left a factory in the Hong Kong area that knew how to make those machines but no one to make them for, until Salton came calling. Salton partnered with this manufacturer to make the Salton machine, and in September of 2003 introduced the Salton coffee brewer to the United States. This happened simultaneously with the launch of a second generation small brewer for $249 from another company, Keurig, available at the time only on the company's website.[2] The Salton brewer was around $59 retail. This was another factor, in addition to Starbucks laying the groundwork for people to thirst after gourmet specialty coffees, in setting the stage for the success of the single-serve coffee brewer.

Because Salton had had such tremendous success with the George Foreman Grill in the early 2000s, they had a very strong reputation with retailers.

When Salton launched its single-cup brewer in the United States, they got the attention of the top executives at the large retail chains. Salton convinced them that this single-cup brewer was the next big thing and was a sure bet. But there was a slight twist in the way that small appliances were usually handled within the big stores. In most cases, appliances were bought by the buyer from the appliance department and then sold in the same department. Food bought for resale, especially in small amounts, was sold in a gourmet food section of the store. The food might be imported bread or coffees or teas.[3]

However, for the Salton one-cup brewer appliance to reach the customers in the strongest way, the coffee brewer and the coffee it brewed would have to be sold in the same department. Salton was putting its money where its coffee brewer was and going full force with television advertising and infomercials. They were really trying to educate consumers about the new concept of brewing a single cup of coffee using the Salton brewing system.[4]

This definitely paved the way for Keurig and its K-Cup, which was not yet a household name.

Nick Lazaris, president of Keurig from 1997 to 2008, notes that when a company like Salton knocks on the door and says this way to make coffee is the next new thing and they are behind it, large retailers will take notice. Salton was able to point to the success of single serve in Europe and say they were the first ones to bring it to the United States. The large retailers listened when Salton told them this new coffeemaker had to be marketed a bit differently.[5]

I have measured out my life with coffee pods.
—As T. S. Eliot might have put it had
The Love Song of J. Alfred Prufrock **been written today**

It wasn't any one thing or event that set the stage for single-serve coffee being taken for granted.

Coffee Enterprises, based in northern Vermont, is an independent coffee testing laboratory certified by the Specialty Coffee Association of America (SCA). They use advanced physical, chemical, and sensory testing equipment, and their senior staff has extensive experience in all aspects and stages of coffee production, from buying and roasting to production to retail operations. They also assist with product development and quality control for single-serve coffees.

Spencer Turer of Coffee Enterprises has experience with coffee quality testing and product development, green coffee sourcing and trading, retail marketing, menu development, and barista training. He is the chairman of the Technical Standards Committee of the SCA, a member of the Technical & Regulatory Affairs Committee of the National Coffee Association USA (NCA), and is a founding member of the Roasters Guild. He is very familiar with the advent of the single serve.[6]

Turer said in an interview that those in the coffee industry knew with the arrival of the single cup—when Keurig and Senseo were launching the single-serve method to brew coffee and even to some extent with the Mellita Pour-Over and the Chemex—it was all about the convenience of making one cup. "The difference," he said, "between the Mellita and the Chemex and the Senseo, the Tassimo, and the Keurig, was when you were dealing with an automatic machine, it was and is all about convenience. Here is a convenient product that enables the user to be able to make a variety of coffee and tea beverages without having to grind and dose and worry about filter paper." And in about forty-five to sixty seconds, you can go from not having anything in your coffee cup and badly wanting a hot beverage, to having that hot beverage in your hand.[7]

The beginning of the consumer version of the single serve was rooted in convenience. But very quickly—strategically speaking; it took a number of years in real time—people started to ask questions, Turer remembers. Coffee drinkers asked, "Why can't it taste better?'" and "Why is it different than what I'm getting in my drip coffee maker?" or "Why does it taste different even though it's the same brands? Why is it different than what I'm getting in the retail stores?"[8]

After everyone got used to the convenience, it became more about the quality. "Quality became a very difficult task," said Turer, "because the hardware of the machine was already established. The size of the machine, the diameter and circumference of the cups, and the spacing, and all the money and resources that had been spent to create these machines, and how pervasive the machines are in the trade. You can't just change them dynamically."[9]

In the single-cup coffee market today, Turer believes, the holy grail seems to be how to provide a convenient product in a cost effective machine that can make a high-quality cup of coffee. Turer advises the clients of Coffee Enterprises that they need to understand the brewing extraction, the contact time, the dosage, the grind, and the filter medium. "There's only so much space in whatever one of these disks, or cups, or packets that you can put coffee in," Turer said. Coffee really blooms when water is added, so you can't just put more coffee in the pod to get more body.

The size of the container is already controlled and finite, and there are a limited number of options available. Many factors have to be taken into account with the single serve—the water temperature, the little bit of pressure, the grind. "You can't grind it too fine or the water's not going to percolate through the grounds," Turer explained.

Turer said they are now seeing companies that are trying to invent something a little bit different, either different technology with the brewing or just completely different dynamics for the cup. And the market is there, he emphasized. "It's a mature market, but it's not the definition we know from generations past, as a mature market . . . there's still emerging growth." In addition, the quality of consumer products today isn't the same as the quality of consumer products from a few generations ago. "You expect your coffee maker to stop working in the twenty-four to thirty-six months, and when it does, you throw it out and you go look for the next best thing. 'What's the highest quality brewer I can buy in my price range?' And if it's something a little bit different, then you do that."

Coffee Enterprises works with a lot of companies regarding brewing technology, and also with many companies regarding Nestlé-type pods, Keurig-type pods, and even with people trying to develop their own types of pods that are a bit different from everything else.[10]

There are many ways to market coffee and there are many ways for the coffee drinker to brew coffee. The single serve fills a need and therefore has a market. "It's the way to get the coffee to the consumer and it has to be the next best thing out there. But really, the Holy Grail in single cup is, it needs to be convenient. It needs to be [an] all-things beverage so it's not just coffee. It's coffee, it's tea, it's fruit products and then if it can do other things as well, that's great. And it has to be cost effective." Turer points out that while coffee made using a single-cup brewer and a pod is less expensive than buying a brewed cup at a retail store, it is dramatically more expensive than buying a pound of coffee and scooping it into your old Melitta.

As we can see from the relatively high price coffee drinkers pay per cup using individual single-serve cups without batting an eye, people will still pay a premium price for a good cup of coffee and the convenience that the single serve provides.

The single serve is here to stay and has become a category of its own in the world of coffee. The National Coffee Association, founded in 1911, was one of the first trade associations for the US coffee industry. Several years ago, the NCA started issuing a separate book just for single serve and they have been publishing one every year because of strong industry interest, according to Joe DeRupo, the NCA's director of External Relations & Communications. Interestingly enough, when they first started noticing single cup, the initial reception was very slow, to the point where they stopped tracking it for a couple of years. It didn't seem like it was going to amount to anything, and then all of a sudden it exploded.

DeRupo said the NCA started tracking single serve as a separate category between 2005 and 2007. The percentages of those who owned a single-cup brewer increased one point each year. The momentum slowed down a bit for a few years and the NCA stopped tracking single serve as a separate category for about three years. "Then," DeRupo added, "we started again in 2011. It was already up to 7 percent." And every year after that, it has gone up significantly. In year—from 2011 to 2016—the figures were 7 percent, then 10 percent, then 12 percent, 15 percent, 27 percent, and 29 percent. That's just for ownership, DeRupo noted.[11]

And, according to DeRupo, single serve will continue to grow: "I think it's still evolving. From 2015 to 2016, it still increased from 27 percent to 29 percent. I don't think it's plateaued."

It is a fact that single-serve coffee has pretty much changed the way we perceive coffee, and it has put a spotlight on the preference of consumers for convenience. The big move toward interest in specialty, or gourmet coffees, and enjoying the variety of different coffees that were made available in the marketplace, led up to that popularity. "We saw that happening for many years," said DeRupo. "Now it seems that convenience is very important."

Also, the timing was right for the single serve to be a hit. It was a way for consumers to try the many different coffee options they saw in the marketplace. Coffee lovers seemed to need as many options as they could get. The more options for having a blissful cup of coffee, the better. There could never be too many blends, roasts, brands, or other choices. Say you come upon a new coffee and want to try a few cups to help decide which roast to get. You can get a small box of their single-serve coffee to experiment with the different roasts.

And with single serve, people could have a different type of coffee any time they wanted. The single-cup brewer enabled coffee drinkers to engage in all the different options with real convenience. Someone could have a Kenyan in the morning, and a Costa Rican in the afternoon, and there was no need to make a full pot. It is just a more convenient way to satisfy the tastes for the wider variety of coffees now available, as DeRupo noted, as well as the preference for convenience.

The NCA doesn't track by brand, but it does track in terms of how many households have a single brewer at home and at work, and how consumers broken out by demographics use their single-serve brewers—at home, away from home, or both.

Single serve grew up as a new technology introduced into the marketplace, DeRupo observed. It had a very slow start, but it has evolved into something longer term, according to the market research the NCA conducted over a long period of time. First came gourmet coffees and people's awareness of them. Then consumers demanded specialty coffees to the extent where the NCA updated the definition of gourmet coffee in their main yearly report, *National Coffee Drinking Trends*. "The single cup brewing report," said DeRupo, "is a breakout from that report, a deep dive into the data on single cup."

Over the years, the NCA saw that they actually had to change their definition of gourmet coffee because it became so commonplace for people to choose premium beans that consumers began to think of gourmet coffee as regular coffee. Gourmet or specialty coffee had become just coffee. What consumers then considered to be gourmet coffee were the "fancy drinks," like lattes and Frappuccinos and the like. "It's evolved to that point where people, first of all, became aware," said DeRupo. "It became very commonplace to look for the gourmet coffee options, then obviously more varieties were made available, and identified, in the marketplace, and people seemed to glom onto all of them." That is the reason, DeRupo thinks, that there is still a lot of elasticity in the marketplace for retail establishments, why there will be a small chain gaining success in a city alongside a Starbucks. The appetite for more and for something different just keeps growing. Coffee's popularity seems to have evolved in waves: Generally speaking, the First Wave of coffee refers to mass-produced coffee and the boom in coffee consumption; the Second Wave is about more specialized coffee and how people regard the beverage; the Third Wave involves considering coffee from cultivation to cup. The definition of Fourth Wave of coffee is a bit more fluid, but according to the musicians of Green Day who are among those in the forefront of this wave [more on that later], the Fourth Wave means sustainability and a real connection to the coffee producers. This is in addition to the drive for quality coffee and emphasis on origin that drove the Third Wave. The single cup is now its own reason for being. "Convenience might have made it grow," said DeRupo, "but without the interest in trying different coffees, that growth may not have been quite as strong."

Single-serve coffee was a technological advancement that came about for convenience, but people eventually tapped into the longer-term trend of trying different coffees, and wanted to partake in different types of coffee at different times of the day, once they understood these choices were out there. "People can now enjoy an excellent cup of coffee with dinner versus something with caffeine in it for breakfast that they [don't] care so much about," said DeRupo, "and this enables them to mix and match and switch off more easily."

> **That's something that annoys the hell out of me—I mean,
> if somebody says the coffee's all ready and it isn't.
> —Holden Caulfield in J.D. Salinger's**
> ***The Catcher in the Rye***

With single serve, the coffee is pretty much always ready.

Nespresso, the Timing Was Not Yet Quite Right

Stepping back in time to 1976, the same year that the Apple computer was created, the first punk rock single was released, and the average price of a new house was less than forty-four thousand dollars, even before the love of specialty coffee became a nationwide obsession, something else was brewing. Something that would lead, eventually, to every coffee lover's dream of brewing a fresh cup of gourmet coffee one cup at a time. Even before anyone was brewing a cup at a time using overgrown tea bag variations, across the ocean someone was at work trying to come up with a single-serve espresso maker. (Some English translations for the Italian word "espresso" include "fast" or "expressed.") Eric Favre, who worked at Nestlé, decided to try his hand at coming up with a faster and easier way to make an admirable espresso. He would eventually come up with the Nespresso system. But in 1976, he was ahead of his time.

With a background in engineering, the Swiss-born Favre was looking for a way to put his skills to work. A trip to Italy set the wheels in motion, as it so often does, for a change in the coffee brewing industry—a faster way to brew high-quality coffee.

In an article in the *Taipei Times*, Favre said that if it had not been for his Italian-born wife, Anna-Maria, he likely would not have come up with the idea for a single-serve coffee capsule. She challenged him to find a better way to make good coffee quickly. According to the article, "In 1975, Favre's coffee quest took him to the Caffe Sant'Eustachio, now listed in travel guides as a place serving one of the best espressos in Rome . . . Using Anna-Maria as his 'spy,' Favre said he discovered that a key to Sant'Eustachio's superior coffee and crema was repeated aeration while hot water was being pumped through the coffee grinds."[12]

Favre's observations led to his idea for a machine that achieved the best possible aeration through a strategically designed single serve. In 1976, while working at Nestlé, Favre invented, patented, and introduced the Nespresso system. He brought his idea and even a prototype of the brewer to his bosses at Nestlé. They were, however, not interested.

It wasn't as if the company was not innovative by nature. Back in 1929 the chairman of Nestlé was asked to find a soluble way to help Brazil make use of an immense surplus of coffee. Relatively crude forms of liquid and crystallized coffee existed, but they were not very appealing. After nearly a decade of very focused research, Nestlé came up with Nescafé in 1938, which they kept improving over the decades.[13] Nestlé was moving forward with its huge success with its new, improved, and bestselling Nescafé instant coffee and was focused on that.[14]

Coming up with a brilliant idea is one thing, but convincing a company to run with it is another. Favre's nascent ideas were a good start, but the timing was just not quite right. A decade later, however, it would be, and Eric Favre would go on to win the Coffee Leaders Lifetime Achievement Award for having a major and lasting effect on the industry.[15]

In the Meantime, Flavia

In 1982, Mars Drinks developed the MARS DRINKS™ FLAVIA® Fresh-brew System for preparing hot drinks using fresh ground coffee and real leaf tea within a single-serve pack. They launched their first Flavia system in 1983 in the United Kingdom and in 1996 in the United States.[16]

Flavia was marketed on the basis of freshness, choice, and convenience. In the United States, it was touted as the first single-serve system that made coffee, tea, and hot chocolate from a single-serve pack. To this day, Flavia is still designed only for the workplace, with thirty-eight products that can be mixed and matched into 150 total combinations.[17]

Produced with corporate clientele in mind, Flavia uses filter packs of fresh coffee that also have a built-in filter. Everything is contained within the compact packet. The filter pack is placed inside a compartment of the brewer. A burst of air opens the sealed packet, followed by pressurized hot water that goes into the packet and brews the coffee. The beverage never comes into contact with the machine, so there is no mess and no cleanup, which is perfect for an office environment. No one has to take responsibility for the coffee area janitorial services.

This has been a very popular option for businesses and there are brewers for a variety of office sizes, starting with the Flavia Creation 150 that suits small offices of fifteen employees or less, on up to the commercial grade Flavia Creation 500 for offices with more than fifty people. The top of the line is the $3,000 Flavia Barista.[18]

Although Flavia is aimed at offices, they have smaller versions available for the workplace, which consumers can purchase from Amazon, office supply sites, and also in some Office Depot and Staples locations.

Nespresso

Eric Favre was not one to give up on his idea for a single-serve brewer that dispensed excellent espresso. He persisted with the bosses at Nestlé and by 1986, Nespresso was born. The coffee was to be encapsulated in little aluminum pods.

In 1988, under the direction of Nestlé chief executive Jean-Paul Gaillard, Nespresso grew and dominates the European market for single serve, as of this writing. Nespresso contracted with Swiss company Turmix in 1990, and then was picked up and marketed by the German company Krups, the Dutch company Philips, the Italian company De'Longhi, and others. Nespresso's espresso-fueled reach was spreading throughout Europe.

Today, Nespresso has found a niche as a single-serve brewer of espresso and also for coffee and runs ads that have featured celebrities like George Clooney, Danny DeVito, Jack Black, Penelope Cruz, and John Malkovich.[19]

Nespresso was always known for authentic espresso and now offers two lines of brewers, the Original Line, which brews espresso, and the VertuoLine, which brews both espresso and coffee. Both use the Nespresso trademark colorful aluminum capsules.

Favre left Nestlé in 1991 to start work on another coffee brewer, and created and patented Monodor, which used a new pod design that did not contain aluminum. He later started yet another new coffee venture, Mocoffee, with cofounder Pascal M. Schittler. Patents for both Monodor and Mocoffee were sold to a Brazilian online wine and beer company.[20]

Favre also used his engineering talents to develop the Tpresso, which, as its name implies, makes fine tea using the capsule method.

When Gaillard left Nestlé, he went on to start a rival to Nespresso and others, his Ethical Coffee Company, another single-serve contender. The only constant about the single-serve business is change and rivalry.

There are two tracks in the development of the single-serve brewer. In the office single-serve coffee is now as ubiquitous as the copy machine. In the home, it is as essential as a microwave.

The single serve represents not just a brewing sea change for the United States' forty billion dollar coffee industry, but also a lifestyle shift. No need for someone to brew a pot of coffee for a family or group. Now you can make fresh-brewed coffee just for yourself, without engaging anyone in conversation, and without even looking up from your iPhone.

CHAPTER 5

The K-Cup,
an Industry Standard

Meanwhile, at the Office

The seeds of another single-serve contender to be reckoned with were starting to germinate in the early 1980s. The ideas for how to find this better way were percolating, but it would be a few years, a few experiments, and a few misses before the idea would become a reality.

No matter how you feel about single-serve coffee, Keurig's rise from a very small company to the behemoth it is now is so noteworthy that there have been case studies about it. Harvard Business School, for example, has used Keurig case studies in its teaching.

Keurig is known for being based on the "razor-blades" model. This utilizes the concept that the razor itself is sold for a low price but the replacement blades are high priced.[1] This is similar to the video game industry where the consoles are relatively inexpensive but the individual games are pricey. Same with some printers. The printers keep going down in price but the ink cartridges are expensive. With this concept, the main proponent, whether brewer, printer, or gaming console, can be sold at a loss and profits can be made by selling the coffee pods, ink cartridges, or games, respectively.

These days the Keurig has become so well-known that it is used as a comparative word when describing something that might be even remotely similar. You can go on the Internet and Google "the Keurig of" and see all sorts of different businesses for beverages and other products: "Not quite the Keurig of beer, PicoBrew brings craft brewing home"[2]; or "The CHiP promises to be the Keurig of Cookies" (that particular article by *Grubstreet* even uses the word Keurig-ify[3]) or "This Handy New Invention Promises to be the Keurig of Cocktails."[4] Keurig has become synonymous with fast and easy. That is an interesting evolution.

Why, spell-check in word processing programs even recognizes the word Keurig. Usually.

But it was not always so.

That name—Keurig. What exactly does it mean, anyway? The word was chosen because it had a European flair and had a Dutch sound to it. In Dutch, *keurig* means "choice," "exquisite," "neat," and "proper," to name a few. But it is also awfully close to the Danish word *krig*, which means war.

The backstory of the Keurig K-Cup includes the idea that there had to be a better way for workers in offices to get decent coffee, no matter what time of day. Inevitably, anyone wandering over to the coffee station would find not a fresh-brewed or even partially palatable pot of coffee but a solidified or burnt mess in the glass pots on the burners because no one in the office wanted to bother cleaning the pots or making a fresh pot. But everyone wanted to have fresh coffee available to drink and to fuel the workday. There had to be a better way.

Getting just the right configuration for practical and palatable fresh-brewed coffee one cup at a time that would make fueling up on java in the office an experience to actually look forward to, would not be easy. How to create a machine that could dispense single cups in a way that was accessible to anyone at the workplace?

What was needed was the right little container to hold the coffee and the right amount of pressure to push just enough water through the tiny container to make a decent cup of coffee, one at a time. Getting just the right formula for both the brewer and coffee container took years. Think about it. Now we are all accustomed to having the widest possible choices of a myriad type of single-serve coffee pods. But a few decades ago nothing like the single serve existed. It wasn't as easy as Honey-I-Shrunk-the-Coffeemaker experimentation.

Matthew Haggerty is an engineer and one of the cofounders of Product Genesis, a strategic management consulting firm. He remembers working with Keurig toward getting the B200 up and ready. Keurig was developing two products, the machine and the K-Cup, and those were two very large initiatives for a start-up to take on.

"People often wonder why start-ups fail so often, and it's because they're so fragile at that stage," Haggerty explained. Getting something to work in the lab can often be a far cry from a manufacturable product, and yet it may not appear that way to the people working on it in the lab.[5]

"When developing a product like this," Haggerty said, "there are usually five developmental phases: experimental, alpha, beta, pre-production, and production. Prior to the experimental stage there is some lab work done to verify certain aspects of the system. Then there's a full-up experimental prototype, which Keurig had, and also an alpha unit or two."

Alphas, said Haggerty, are usually a good stab at what the devices look like and how they work, and they meet all the performance requirements: "There might be anywhere from ten to 100 Betas, depending on the intended volume of manufacture, they would be put into places close by. The pre-production phase would be the first full-on manufacturing run, but there are still going to be things to learn in the early fielding of these units. Field service, corrective action, reporting and things like that are still important."

Dick Sweeney had a background in engineering and he came onboard at Keurig because he was interested in the idea of single-serve coffee for the office environment. It made sense. If companies could keep their workers in the office by offering them delicious and fueling coffee, instead of the them going out for decent-tasting coffee, a lot of work hours would be saved and efficiency would increase. Employees could enjoy cups of great quality coffee while at work, too.

Sweeney knew the mechanical end of things. Said Sweeney, "Two things hit me, one was the single-serve portion pack, which I'd seen, but there hadn't been anything I considered really good out there. What was more intriguing was the office coffee service market which I'd never given a thought to." The office coffee service market was very appealing because it has a low cost of entry, as opposed to standard retail where there is a great deal of advertising and promotion expense. "That was enticing," recalls Sweeney. And before long, Sweeney became a cofounder with Keurig. "We worked on the product and raised money for development and it got venture capital money in '95."[6]

It was Sweeney's job to figure out a way to automate the production of the machine. He had the product development and manufacturing experience. Nailing the prototype was one thing, but how could they cost-effectively produce in large quantities?

What surprised Sweeney about the whole process was the level of complexity involved: "The architecture of the system, whether it's ours or anybody else's, they're all the same. Essentially you have to have a portion pack, an appliance that will efficiently utilize the portion pack in a way that's very simple for the consumer, and then you need a packaging automation to make, in the beginning, thousands, tens of thousands, now billions, of portion packs." The portion pack itself, which makes the Keurig system unique, has a controlled atmospheric environment. That simply means that they flush the cup with nitrogen during production to drive out the oxygen because oxygen will make the coffee go stale. Such a new concept was a leap of faith. Sweeney is not a marketing person but he thinks Keurig's success comes from the fact that they got the North American consumer used to drinking a fresh cup of coffee consistently every time, something that coffee drinkers do not always get with drip coffee. Keurig's marketing strategy to break into the office coffee market was well-thought-out and planned.[7]

Another person familiar with Keurig's expansion, although he was not part of the development team, is Jeff Hovis, who was the director of Business Development at Product Genesis at the time.

Keurig partnered with regional coffee roasters who already had a presence in their local markets, Hovis notes. These partnerships with regional roasters were the way for Keurig to get the attention of the big national players. So while Green Mountain Roasters was the obvious first partner and investor, with coverage in the Northeastern States, they realized that they could only provide so much market access. So they allowed Keurig to pursue other regional players like Van Houtte in Canada, Caribou in the Western United States, Tully's on the West Coast, Diedrich in the Rocky Mountain region, and Timothy's in Ontario Canada.[8]

An engineer who worked on the commercial brewer even before Product Genesis came onboard, Rick Beaulieu was one of the original people Keurig hired to work on the design. While there were two basic arms of activity, he said, one being the brewer and the other the packaging line—he ended up working on both—the brewer was his primary responsibility. He was involved in redesigning the original prototype into what became the B2000.[9]

There were, understandably, difficulties along the way. As with most start-ups, there was the challenge of getting everything done by a specified date. Product development is problematic when it comes to a timeline because it really does not lend itself to a predictable schedule. Unforeseen issues can come up. "You're struggling to overcome these problems that aren't really clear when you first discover them," Beaulieu said, "and you don't exactly know what the right answer is until you've actually tried and tested it, etc."

At the root of everything—because of the nature of the business—is that those who have a financial stake don't really care about problems; they just care about having the product ready by the date they were promised. Another element of this particular project that was significant was the disposable component that had to be consistently manufactured.[10]

And the brewer had to accommodate both: "The brewer and all its variants have to accommodate all the variations that can come out of the packaging line." This was the kind of design problem that Keurig's early developers had to wrestle with and manage.

Some pieces of the puzzle that were especially complicated were getting the brewing time as short as possible so that no one waited too long for their coffee, as well as preventing carryover between different coffees, particularly complex if somebody is trying to brew a flavored coffee and the next person wants regular coffee.

Precise temperature control was critical to getting a small amount of coffee to brew properly in a fast timeframe. Engineering tests were performed as well as quite a few tests to find the balance between brewing coffee and creating a successful and fast single serve.

To ensure that there was no carryover of flavors from one brew cycle to the next, in the original Keurig brewer, an air blast occurred between servings. It was like a slug of air clearing out the line so that fluid would not continuously sit in the line.

The number one priority for the first commercial Keurig brewer was that it had to brew coffee fast. There was a lot of perception testing with potential users to get a sense of "Is this brewing fast enough to be credible? Will somebody wait this long for a cup of coffee rather than pouring it out of a pot?" Getting that cycle time down to what was within people's perception of "That's a reasonable amount of time to wait for a cup of coffee" was critical.

The original B2000 was an amazingly durable product. Hovis says they actually had that unit in their office up until about 2013, so the machine was about fifteen years old.

Something that still stands out in Hovis's mind is that no one had a clue how big single-serve coffee would be: "The original concept was 'Oh, could we knock off office brewers' and in a big office environment, people will pay for this." People in the office wouldn't have to think about how long the pot of sludge that once was coffee was sitting on the burner.

Office workers could have coffee that was always fresh, no matter what time it was. The idea that single-serve brewers, and Keurig brewers in particular, would get to the point of being a major consumer appliance and that a huge fraction of the population would get their coffee this way, was pretty much inconceivable. Product Genesis was not involved with the manufacture of the consumer brewer.

Money

Finding investors to fund the operation was not easy. According to Dick Sweeney, the operation was self-funded from 1993 until 1995. They had an initial patent for the K-Cup so that gave them something tangible to bring to investors along with prototypes that sometimes would work and sometimes would spill hot water all over conference room tables.

But they weren't getting the investors they needed to fund the new product. Things were getting tense, with money drying up and an uncertainty about the future of the invention growing, no matter how innovative it was.

And it wasn't for lack of trying or commitment. They took the product on road shows, not knowing whether the prototype pods would brew a stellar cup of coffee or a cup of coffee grounds-laden liquid, or whether the pods would rupture and leak all over the furniture of the venture capitalists being courted. They were met with a lot of negative reactions—they were told it would never take off, that no one would buy it.

At the eleventh hour in 1994 they found an investor, the Food Fund, and the very long slog resulted in Keurig, the company that set the standards for the single serve with their brewers and K-Cups. What led the first investor to invest in the nascent single-serve coffee start-up? John Trucano was with Food Fund at the time. He said that the main thing was that most people were dissatisfied with their office coffee—it sat on a burner all day and people could not get what they wanted, a good-tasting, keep-me-going single cup of fresh coffee. He thought that because each person could have whatever individual type of coffee they wanted, this made a lot of sense. He hadn't realized all the technical hurdles that had to be overcome, and it was not easy.[11]

But Trucano knew a product like this had what it took to do really, really well. "I think the main thing was I just talked to enough people [who] were very unhappy with their office coffee," he said. "This was about the time when Starbucks and Caribou and all these were developing these stores with gourmet coffee, and more and more people were stopping there and bringing a cup into their office rather than having the office coffee that they didn't like."

Trucano mentally calculated what people were paying for a cup of coffee at gourmet coffee shops. He figured that more and more people were paying $1.00, $1.50, and up for a cup (at the time . . . that would seem like a bargain now!) of Starbucks to bring to the office rather than drink a free cup at the office because they weren't happy with the quality of the office coffee. So he reasoned that if this coffee brewer could really make a premier cup of coffee it made sense that it would do well.

Quite a few unexpected and unforeseen issues regarding investing came up with this developing product. For instance, according to Trucano, the two biggest hurdles were finding an engineering company to design a machine that could produce K-Cups at high speed. The first company that they contracted with did not work out. Trucano and Sweeney found a company in Minnesota that designed a machine that produced one hundred cups a minute. "It really took a combination of finding a machine that could make these K-Cups at high speed," Trucano said, "and then also find all the intricacies within the brewer to make sure that we could make the brewer work, and this took several years."

As to how they found a manufacturer that could handle churning out a high number of K-Cups at a time, Trucano says that this manufacturer had made a packaging line for a company that he knew very well in the microwave popcorn business, and so he thought they would be able to overcome the engineering hurdles to quickly make a large quantity of cups. Trucano mentioned that he and Sweeney talked to them about the need to put a filter paper inside the cup, sonic weld it to the top, put coffee in it, and then put a top on it. "We explained it to them, and they said, 'Yeah, we think we can do that. It will cost you $750,000, but we think we can make one that can do a hundred a minute.' It took them about a year, but they were able to do it. Without that, we were dead."

It would take years and a lot of money pouring in to get the whole single-serve brewing system just right. To give an idea of how difficult this process was, below is an overview of the money expended prior to the company earning any revenue:

1994—$50,000
1995—$1,000,000
1996—$1,000,000
1997—$1,000,000
1998—$4,000,000[12]

Trucano said that the initial $50,000 was for legal fees to file patents on the brewer process and the K-Cup design, and also a little money for the two founders to live on, since they had invested everything they had into the start-up. "These patents were issued in 1995 and were good for seventeen years until 2012 when competition was allowed to compete in the K-Cup business."

They had limited funds and had to rely on other investors to help them or they could never have gotten this done, Trucano said. There was a venture fund in Boston that co-invested with them, but, according to Trucano: "The Food Fund itself only put about a million dollars in, but we had contacts in Minneapolis that put another seven million dollars in."

The logistics involved in putting together the whole package of the brewer were complicated. There were a few times Trucano and the Food Fund wondered about their odds of success. He said that there were times when they came pretty close to walking away from the whole thing. At the end of 1996, they still really didn't have a brewer that worked, they didn't have a K-Cup line that worked, and as a group they were over two million dollars into the deal. "But I think because we still thought there was a huge potential, we decided to give it another round of financing," Trucano said. Trucano even went along on some of the early road shows to drum up interest in this new way to make coffee.

From Trucano's standpoint, Food Fund's investment in Keurig at such an early stage was probably the earliest point at which he had ever invested in a company. Things were really in the research and development stage.

It was tough going at the very beginning. One time, according to Trucano, the team went to Minneapolis for a demo for some potential investors there. They put the K-Cups in the machine and the cups blew up. It turns out that on the airplane trip to Minneapolis something happened with the pressure in the K-Cups so they literally exploded in the brewer. Every time they thought they had one thing worked out, Trucano remembered, something else would crop up.

But when they finally had the office brewer ready to go, it quickly became the number one office single-serve coffee brewer. People liked the fact that they had a brand name and that the K-Cups contained well-known and well-liked named coffees. In the Northeast the K-Cups contained Green Mountain, in the Midwest, Caribou, all names of coffee purveyors that people trusted and coffee people would want to drink. the K-Cups contained exciting for coffee lovers who worked in offices.

People in offices would love and welcome a great cup of coffee at work. But would convincing office managers to install the Keurig in the workspace be an easy or hard sell? The convenience and apportionment of brewing using the single-serve system was going to cost more. That was just the way it was. Helping the decision makers in the offices understand and accept that idea was a bit of a challenge. The team had to convince office managers that they should pay forty cents for a cup of coffee, when they were making twelve-cup pots that cost between a nickel and a dime per cup, Trucano explains. But because there's a lot of waste and a lot of cleanup with the traditional office coffee setup with glass coffee pots and loose grounds, the team was able to convince the people in charge of purchasing the coffee systems that paying forty cents was not that much because they were paying five to ten cents for a bad cup of coffee, and probably half of it was being thrown out.[13]

Trucano said that taking the Keurig to the next level, to the home environment, was really a decision that was made because a lot of people in the offices said they wanted to have the same appliance for their home. This meant reengineering the brewer yet again, since it had to be made smaller because it was too big for most kitchen counters. They contracted with a firm in Boston to downsize the basic machine into one that could fit on a home counter.

Getting the Keurig system out in the consumer marketplace was difficult without distribution in big stores like Walmart, Target, and so on. Initially, remembers Trucano, they relied on placards set up near the Keurig machines in the offices that said, "If you want one of these for your home, go on Keurig.com and you can order the machine and then you can also order the K-Cups." No one wanted people to abscond with K-Cups from the office and take them home.

CHAPTER 6

The Nascent Keurig and the K-Cup

Nick Lazaris became president and CEO of Keurig in February 1997 and took the company to the next level. Lazaris had been recruited to be the new president and CEO by the venture capitalists who, at that point, owned a controlling interest in the company. The venture capitalists basically told the young company that they would support them for one year to get the product to market. According to Lazaris, the company was five years old at the time he joined it, and had not yet realized success with commercializing the concept of single cup.[1]

Lazaris said there were two venture capital firms, the larger of the two being MDT Advisors, and the other was the aforementioned Food Fund, the small company focused on food and beverage out of Minnesota.[2] After the initial investment, there was a second round of investment from the venture capitalists. With this second round of financing, the venture capitalists acquired majority ownership of the company and as such, were not happy with the progress being made toward commercializing the product. When Lazaris was recruited to be the new CEO there were about eight employees at the time.[3]

Lazaris had been the CEO of the oldest photo frame company in the United States. They sold products that were design sensitive through department stores and independent retailers, so he understood the retail channels. Before that, Lazaris was a VP of marketing with a company called Wright Line, and worked with a sales force, so he also had experience with sales, marketing, and general management in both business-to-business and in consumer products.

Keurig was, on its front end, a business-to-business product that had already been introduced to the office segment for office coffee, Lazaris recalled. From the moment he interviewed for the CEO job, the idea was, if Keurig could make it as the coffee used in the office environment, they would have a home run, and if they could figure out a way to make it into consumer products, they would have a grand slam. So, Lazaris signed on.

There were problems getting it out in the marketplace. The first thing clearly that "had to be done or nothing else follows" was the product needed to be commercialized. The Keurig is, as Lazaris explained, a system product. It's the combination of a K-Cup and a Keurig brewer, like other system products; i.e., the Nespresso has the Nespresso capsule. This involves three things. It involves a brewer, which can work with a K-Cup and produce a controlled amount of water at a certain temperature and pressure to brew the coffee. It involves the K-Cup itself, and then the third component is the machine that makes the K-Cups. "For a startup to take on those challenges is not an easy thing," said Lazaris.

Keurig found some outside engineering partners to help the handful of engineers the company had to work on the brewer. They redesigned the product that had been developed to date, as Lazaris explained. "We essentially wrote off, threw away, and started over."

Keurig hired engineers to work on the new brewer, and engineers to work on the new packaging line. "Those two things," said Lazaris, "had to come together in twelve months' time, and of course the K-Cup that was produced on that packaging line had to work effectively with the brewer. Much like the razor-razorblade, you needed the razorblade to go in the razor, but you needed a machine to make the razorblade. These [were] not easy challenges."

There was much work to do before Keurig could hope to succeed as a brand and as a company. "Technically, we had a set of challenges that needed to be overcome before anything could happen," said Lazaris. "That [was] number one. Number two was the business model." When Lazaris arrived at the company, the business model was fundamentally oriented toward Keurig going after the office coffee market using not only its own brewer but its own brand of K-Cups. Keurig would not only make the brewer and the K-Cups, Keurig would have its own brand of coffee in the K-Cups, instead of a more recognized brand like, say, Green Mountain.

After Lazaris joined the company, he and the management team came up with a different business model. Instead of having someone manufacture the K-Cups for Keurig on a contract basis with Keurig selling them to distributors, they determined that it would be more effective and efficient to have that contract manufacturer be a branded gourmet coffee roaster and take ownership of the product. When the contract manufacturer sold the product to Keurig's licensed distributors, Keurig would receive a royalty. It was a different structure, Lazaris observed. It eliminated the inefficiencies of Keurig having to handle and own the inventory. Secondly, it also gave them the ability to piggyback on the reputation of the brand of the coffee roaster to introduce Keurig's technology into the marketplace. It was, he said, "Sort of like a halo effect."[4]

Keurig entered the office coffee market on January 19, 1998, within twelve months of Lazaris joining the company. They launched in the Boston area as well as New York, and pretty soon thereafter, they were in the mid-Atlantic states. "That was our focus the first year," Lazaris said. When the distributors they partnered with would call on potential offices, they could say, "We have this new technology that brews one cup at a time, and it uses Green Mountain coffee." Green Mountain had brand recognition in that part of the country.

This certainly helped generate tangible interest in the system. "Once we got the door open and the demonstrations were done, we did have a really neat technology that let people enjoy the coffee variety they wanted.

It allowed the employer to enjoy the benefits of people staying in the office as opposed to going out to get their gourmet coffee, etc."

This was a big part of Keurig's appeal in the workplace. Sure, having a variety of recognizable and loved coffees available in K-Cups whenever an employee wanted a fresh cup of coffee would help to keep workers more content. But having the single-serve gourmet coffee option right there in the office also meant that workers would likely make fewer trips outside of the office to trek to the closest specialty coffee shop. In theory, both management and employees would be happy. Employees would have access to gourmet coffee right there in the office so they would spend more time in the office, which would please employers. Office managers would also have less coffee preparation mess to delegate for clean up.[5]

Keurig's business model really affected their long-term growth. Keurig became, as Lazaris pointed out, a platform technology for gourmet coffee roasters to be able to offer their coffee into a channel that they really didn't have distribution in, which was office coffee. The reason they didn't have distribution is they hadn't wanted it in the past. Having their coffee available for brewing in the usual office coffee system could leave their brand image vulnerable, as Lazaris explained. Let's say, for example, that Green Mountain coffee had been available for employees to brew using the old coffee systems. This could leave Green Mountain's brand vulnerable because when people brewed coffee and left that quarter or half pot of coffee burning on the coffeemaker, the taste of the coffee was ruined. People would then say, "Boy, that Green Mountain coffee doesn't taste good," when the reason it didn't taste good was because it had been stewing into a sludge for hours.

The coffee rosters wanted to be in the channel, but they didn't have an effective way of doing it until Keurig came along and made office coffee available for, first Green Mountain and, then, a number of coffee roasters across the country. "That's how we went after the office coffee market," he said, "obviously picking the right distributors, training them on how to sell and how to service, all that was very important."

There were some problems getting distributors interested in putting the Keurig in offices. Lazaris recalled that the distributors did not like Keurig's economic model. In the first place, Keurig did not want to give anybody an exclusive. Keurig had a couple of competitors in the market at the time. Keurig was not the first in the offices or in the homes with what was technically a single-serve version. The first was a company called FilterFresh. The FilterFresh system worked with one or two coffee hoppers into which the coffee was poured, and with the press of a button, the machine would meter the coffee into a chamber, provide hot water, and pump the coffee through filter paper, and you'd have a freshly brewed cup of coffee. Lazaris said, "We would call that coffee 'fresh brewed stale coffee' because when the coffee's in the hopper, it gets stale and there wasn't much in the way of selection." That passed for single serve at the time.[6]

There also was that other single cup competitor—MARS DRINKS™ FLAVIA®.

They were in the market two years ahead of Keurig with a single-cup system that used a different patented technology that works with packets instead of little cups. The basic concept was the same; pressurized hot water, puncturing a packet, putting that pressurized hot water in the packet to brew the coffee, and pushing it through a filter into your cup. There are some differences though. Flavia's brewing system prevents cross-contamination of flavors since whatever is in the packet—coffee, tea, hot chocolate—never comes into contact with the machine.[7]

So Keurig had competitors in the market already, and those competitors had, at the time, a set of exclusive distributors, meaning there was one in each geographical territory. Keurig went to market with a different idea: a 'select but nonexclusive' relationship with distributors. When Keurig launched on January 19, 1998, in New York City, they had two, and pretty soon three, distributors in New York, two in Boston, and two in Rhode Island. "We did not believe that there should be one distributor in any city because we thought the market was too big. Having more than one distributor was good for both distributors because it would help build the awareness of the product. That was number one," Lazaris said.

According to Lazaris, the distributors were used to making 50 percent or more gross margin on any coffee product they sold. He said, "With Keurig, their gross margin was more like 33 percent, 35 percent. They said, 'This doesn't satisfy our business model.' To which we responded, 'When you go to the bank, you don't take percent, you take cents. If you place a Keurig brewer, you will earn three times per cup what you're making today. You'll earn 15 cents a cup instead of five cents a cup. If all you do is place Keurig in offices and don't increase the number of cups, it's the same number of cups, you'll triple your profit. You won't make 50 percent gross margin because if you did, the price would be too high.' Of course they set their own prices, but when there's more than one distributor, there's a bit of competition and it keeps prices from getting so high there's no market."

Keurig found the right distributors, said Lazaris, and they were generally smaller single-owner distributorships and were more entrepreneurial. They used the Keurig product for new account generation, and they did very well: "As soon as they were making money, other people wanted to be a distributor of ours. In a few years, we were bringing on board regional distributors who covered more than one city and had multiple offices. Probably three or four years after we launched, we were now working with national distributors like Aramark, together with regional and local mom and pops."

Over the course of two to three years, Keurig expanded distribution from the East Coast all the way across the United States and then across the border into Canada. New distributors came on board as time went on, including bottled water distributors and office products distributors in addition to office coffee distributors. "There were many ways for people to make money selling Keurig," he says, "and for office employees to enjoy having the Keurig option. People really did like our product."

Then came the dot-com implosion in March 2000, where the Nasdaq dropped 78 percent over thirty months, and a lot of companies started cutting back. Keurig had a good position with a lot of technology companies, and with the dot-com bust those companies were cutting back on employees, as well as employee benefits. Lazaris heard stories about the Keurig brewer starting to be wheeled out of an office and the employees subsequently complaining. The employees felt that since there were fewer of them and they would be working a lot harder, they needed good coffee nearby now more than ever and they wanted the Keurig. Keurig managed to hold their position in the marketplace and came back even stronger as the economy recovered.[8]

Not only did the brewer have to be great, but so did the coffee in the single-serve pods. Green Mountain Coffee, which had been lusting after a bigger share in the premium coffee market, invested a 35 percent stake in Keurig in 1996.[9]

Summing up, Keurig's number one challenge was getting the product right. The number two challenge was getting their go-to market strategy right, and the third challenge was training their distributors to go out and sell, and also developing their distribution structure. By their third year, Keurig was a profitable enterprise with great prospects, and that's when they started to take a good look at the consumer market.[10]

A Home Version of the Keurig Takes Shape

Keurig was getting close to having a brewer ready for home use. While this would be a new market, the idea to get the Keurig into the home had been there for a while. When Nick Lazaris was interviewing with the venture capital firm in late 1996, it was obvious that they had a product that "fundamentally, even though it was targeted for offices, was going to be used by coffee drinkers. Consumers."[11]

There were a few reasons for the expansion into the consumer market. One reason, of course, had to do with the management of the business. But another reason for going over to the consumer side was that it would please the employees of offices that used the commercial Keurig.

"We always understood there was a consumer market potential," said Lazaris, "but I'll have to say that early on, it was clear that significant accomplishments had to occur before we could ever get in the consumer market. One of them was the size and cost of the brewer."

The original Keurig commercial brewer cost over $700. They knew that a brewer needed to be, at most, a couple hundred dollars in the consumer market, so they needed a revolution in their thinking for a different generation of machine. Then they needed to figure out how they were going to create consumer awareness and traction so that people would try their product and then buy the brewer for home use. Would consumers be willing to pay 50 cents or more per cup of coffee to have fresh brewed coffee at home? Coffee in the office is generally free, so these were really significant hurdles.[12]

When they were ready to move into the consumer market, Keurig needed to get a brewer manufactured and have the retail cost be around $150. At that point there were a few well-heeled competitors, including Phillips' and Sara Lee's Senseo, for instance, which used a plastic-free coffee pod in its brewer and was launched in the Netherlands in 2001. Philips made the brewer while the coffee pods were distributed by Sara Lee.[13]

The concept of single cup was already present in the commercial market for filtered coffee, and already present in the consumer markets for espresso, and then came the Philips-Sara Lee Senseo system, which followed the initial launch in the Netherlands with promotion in Belgium, France, Germany, Austria, Denmark, United Kingdom, United States, and Australia, in that order.[14] A lot of US companies kept a close eye on the Senseo, which came to the United States in 2005. "What happened," said Lazaris, "was the product was very well received by consumers in [the Netherlands], and the structure that Douwe Egberts [Philips' coffee brand] and Sara Lee set up for pod distribution through grocery made the pods easily available."

So the Senseo had easy availability of the pods, the price of the brewer was agreeable to consumers, and people liked the machine. The launch of the Senseo attracted a lot of attention in the US market. Procter and Gamble started looking at developing a pod system for the United States and in 2004 launched a single-serve brewer, Home Café, which used soft pods not unlike the Senseo's.[15] Sara Lee and Philips, in the meantime, focused on European distribution.

The idea for single-serve coffee was so well-timed that a lot of other companies jumped into the market for making pods. The way it usually works is that the company has to sell the coffee brewer at a loss but make it up by selling the pods for the brewer. In any case, the market for single-serve coffee was getting a little messy. While the Senseo grew very quickly, the brewer wasn't launched in the United States right away. The first single-cup pod coffee machine for home use in the United States was brought out by Salton.

Salton Leads the Way

Nick Lazaris views Salton's release of a single-serve brewer as a good thing, a very good thing for Keurig. Why, when it would seem that Salton beat Keurig to the single-serve punch? If it wasn't for Salton, he explained, Keurig could never have opened those doors with the retailers; Keurig was just not that known. But when somebody like Salton says this is the next big thing and they are behind it, and they can point to its success in Europe, that is different. Salton also told the retailers that this appliance would have to be marketed differently. "They could say that to the people who could make the changes in those retail organizations so as to support the launch," he pointed out.

When Salton decided to bring out a single-cup brewer in the United States, recalled Lazaris, their people were able to go to the senior levels of retail executives of the big chains to talk to them. They could tell the top executives that this was the next wave and that they could be a partner but they would have to do something a bit differently than they'd done before, as explained earlier. It was a system and had to be promoted and sold as a system.

In February of 2004, Procter and Gamble announced that it was launching its own pod system called Home Café, also to be sold to retailers.[16] So, remembers Lazaris, the retailers were going to have two lines of single-serve brewers to choose from. But wait. There's more. Sara Lee and Philips were bringing Senseo to the United States in the fall of 2004.

So by the time one year had elapsed, three different pod systems were in the United States, and then there was a fourth—Keurig. Keurig's head of the at-home division went out in January 2004 knowing that Salton was in the market, and knowing that Procter and Gamble and Sara Lee were coming, Lazaris said. He called on the retailers and told them that since they'd already started selling single cup brewers, they must believe that it was going to be a big industry. The idea was to convince the executives at the big stores to go with Keurig instead of their competitors.[17]

Lazaris said they explained to the heads of the retail outlets that while stores were probably already considering adding one or both of the Home Café and Senseo systems, and Keurig's brewers cost two or three times as much as the competitors and their coffee cost twice as much, they really ought to try Keurig too, because Keurig was different. Keurig had a different concept that provided a better cup of coffee that a significant percent of the store's customers would want to upgrade to. They told the heads of the stores that every time they sold a Keurig brewer for $149, they would be making three times the gross profit dollars that they made selling a Salton brewer at $49. And the stores would be making twice as much with the coffee. They asked, "If you could just give us some stores to test in, in holiday 2004, and allow us to demonstrate our machine, you'll see that Keurig outsells everybody else."

Keurig was in two hundred stores of ten retailers in 2004. This was the third generation of the brewer that used a new set of patents to lower the cost. "While we did sell at a loss, it was a small loss," Lazaris said. They launched the product in November 2004 at select retailers, and they supported the introduction with in-store demonstrations. "The product was high quality," he said, "so anybody that saw the packaging or better yet, touched the machine, saw the machine, saw the finish, saw the fit, let alone tasted the coffee from the machine, saw that it was superior to the alternatives and we sold through very well. The retailers liked us."

By the next holiday season, Keurig was in 3,500 stores.

That is when Kraft's Tassimo system was launched in the United States. The Tassimo system used fully encapsulated pods similar to what the Keurig used, albeit of a different shape. While the folks at Keurig might say that the coffee pillow-shaped Senseo pods were all a bit messy and allowed for taste contamination, and so on, the same could not be said of the Tassimo system. The Tassimo also offered options for making lattes and cappuccinos using the pods. "Of course we were concerned about that because they had a portion pack that had an irradiated liquid milk in it," said Lazaris. In the end, consumers in the United States seemed more interested in having a large variety of coffees. Keurig offered sixty K-Cup varieties when they launched. Over the course of the next couple years, that increased to hundreds.

Since there were several different types of single-serve brewers when Keurig brought out its commercial Keurig, consumers were already aware of single-serve options because of all of the advertising from the other brands. Said Lazaris, "Our strategy was, let our competitors educate the public and get them in the store, that's where our demonstration and our packaging, and the look and feel of the product need to stand out so they buy from us, and we capture those customers."

An important part of the strategy of the single-serve brewing system is, of course, the coffee. Sara Lee's and Procter & Gamble's coffee pods were available in thousands of grocery stores across the country. Since that is where people shopped for coffee, it seemed like a sure thing. They already had the channel for the coffee. They just needed to sell a huge number of machines through the retailers to create demand to pull those coffee pods off of the supermarket shelves.[18]

Keurig at the time had no grocery store relationships, so they were able to tell the department store retailers that not only were they going to make money selling the brewer and the initial set of K-Cups, but people would have to keep returning to their store to buy more K-Cups. Keurig was offering K-Cups on the Internet as well, particularly varieties that retailers didn't offer.[19] As Lazaris said, they told the retailers, "You'll have long term benefit from K-Cups." He continued, "But nobody realized just how big a business the K-Cup business would be for department and specialty stores. Retailers like Bed Bath & Beyond did a huge business in K-Cups."

This meant that in the beginning Keurig did not have to be concerned about having K-Cups in thousands of stores; they just needed to have the K-Cups in the stores that sold the brewers so people always knew they could buy them there, or they could go on the Internet and buy directly from Keurig.[20] "That allowed us to more gradually grow our in-store base, which we did, to get to the tipping point that then starts to justify grocery store distribution, which we watched," Lazaris said. "We knew the zip codes of the people who bought our product and who shopped with us."

Green Mountain acquired Keurig in 2006 and was well positioned to begin putting K-Cups into stores where the company felt that the population had enough machines to make the risk worthwhile, which it did. "We had an ability to grow more slowly and deliberately. It didn't have to be a grand slam in the first inning of the game," Lazaris said.

Gradually, over the years, grocery store distribution has become the key channel for Keurig K-Cups. "It was a different kind of approach toward the marketplace," added Lazaris, "and as a startup and later on as part of Green Mountain, a small company, one has to be resourceful, and we were."

Fast forward briefly to 2015 and Keurig Green Mountain is bought by an investor consortium led by JAB Holdings, which also own Peet's Coffee, Caribou Coffee, Stumptown Coffee Roasters, and coffee giant Jacobs Douwe Egberts, as well as a majority stake in Intelligentsia Coffee. JAB Holdings manages the money of the Reimann family, one of the world's richest families. [21, 22]

CHAPTER 7

K-Cup, Etcetera

The My K-Cup Option

One product development and go-to market strategy was to connect the coffees that consumers wanted with the Keurig. When Keurig launched the retail version of their brewer, they surveyed customers to find out what they wanted in a single-serve brewer. According to Lazaris, they found out early on with their studies that sometimes people wanted a variety or brand of coffee that wasn't being offered in a K-Cup. A couple could be interested in buying a Keurig brewer for their home, but one half of the couple really had to have their morning Starbucks, for example, while the other couldn't live without a morning cup of Dunkin' Donuts coffee.[1]

Keurig featured numerous brands of coffee, including at least one gourmet brand, on the brewer boxes. They were always adding brands in the beginning so it was important to have at least one recognizable quality brand on the box that people all over the country would know.

When Keurig launched, they had about a dozen brands. Keurig started to hear objections from people that their reason for not buying a brewer was because they did not see their favorite brand on the box. "That's when we internally developed the My K-Cup," Lazaris said. "My K-Cup is a two-part piece of plastic that lets you put your own coffee in. You can pop the K-Cup holder out, put the My K-Cup in, brew your own coffee."

They did some market testing before they launched the My K-Cup because they wanted to find out how often people would use it. They found that people did not use it very often. When people had the My K-Cup, they liked it and knew how to use it, but fundamentally they greatly preferred the convenience of putting a K-Cup in the brewer and pressing the button.[2]

But, just the same, Lazaris said they felt pretty confident that if they merchandised the My K-Cup, either with the brewer or separately, people would understand that they weren't locked into the Keurig system and they could use any coffee they wanted. Secondly, it removed a significant hesitation to buying Keurig, and third, he said, "Once that person was in Keurig, the person in the couple who wanted to use their own coffee, after a little bit of exploration, which is why we provided assortment packs, would find another brand that was close enough, and the convenience factor trumped everything else."

The My K-Cup helped Keurig sell a lot of brewers, according to Lazaris, and they developed a strong relationship with their customers, who did a lot of advertising by word of mouth.[3] Customers liked being able to offer friends who came to dinner choices of coffees and teas.

And the My K-Cup offered a more environmentally friendly way to brew coffee for one.

An Analyst's View of Keurig in the Early Years

Scott Van Winkle, who followed Keurig when he was an analyst with Canaccord Genuity, said that in the early days, Keurig was one of the few if not the only publicly traded company like it. There were, of course, Nespresso as a part of Nestlé, Kraft and its Tassimo, and Starbucks, which launched Verismo, their own product, but there wasn't really a publicly traded company that competed with Keurig.[4]

"I think any time you have the success that they had, I mean really changing how consumers made coffee," Van Winkle explained, "not just taking share from other coffee makers, but literally changing the way consumers make coffee, and you build this installed base of users, you're going to get challenged . . ." Van Winkle thinks that it's natural that any company that dominates a market like Keurig is going to attract competition that is going to try and go around them in one way or another. Keurig was building a business and signing up partners in the early days, like Green Mountain Coffee, Timothy's World Coffee, and Diedrich Coffee for a while before Green Mountain bought them in 2009.[5]

Keurig would sign up coffee partners and have them do a lot of the marketing from the standpoint of their brands, putting up capital for building packaging facilities. Tying up partnerships ultimately became the best defense of their system and it was so successful that they eventually signed Folgers, Kraft, Dunkin' Donuts, and Starbucks.

While there was debate on Wall Street about the competition that Keurig would generate,[6] Van Winkle pointed out that when you've partnered with the brands that dominate the coffee industry, you've reduced the risk of your intellectual property not holding up.

Regarding entering the consumer market, Van Winkle said, "I don't think at that point I had any expectation that the consumer piece was going to be significant. It was promising, it was an opportunity, but it hadn't been realized."

There were, of course, lots of challenges to Keurig and its achievement as often happens when a product is that successful. But Keurig kept improving the system, and the quality of the coffee started to improve, and the advancements proved the naysayers on Wall Street who said that "the coffee wasn't good enough" or "the coffee wasn't hot enough," wrong. There was, he added, the cost of the low-end machine. The thinking was that "Consumers aren't going to do this when they're used to spending twenty dollars for a Mr. Coffee," he remembered.[7]

But the practicality just could not be beat. It changed the game. In the early days there were lots of issues to overcome, Van Winkle pointed out, like price and consistency of taste—it's different with a slow-drip coffeemaker versus brewing it in forty seconds: "The simple rule is the more time the hot water spends on the coffee grounds, the more it tastes like coffee. So at the beginning I would say it was more perception that they couldn't overcome the issues, and then in each subsequent improvement, it became dramatically better and today the quality of the coffee coming out of one of those machines is pretty darn good."

About the 2.0 Controversy

Van Winkle thinks that the initial plan for the 2.0 Keurig brewer was to have more interactivity between the machine and the cup. The idea was that it would benefit the consumer since the he or she could brew the coffee as needed for each K-Cup. Maybe one particular coffee needed to be brewed for forty-five seconds rather than thirty-five. There would be real interactivity, he said, and that was the argument for the consumer.[8]

He does not think that the 2.0, from the standpoint of the company, was an effort to defend their market share of the pods compatible with the machine. The reality of the 2.0 was that there was just some coloring on the top of the label that the machine read, and as soon as that was figured out, there were hacks to circumvent it, on YouTube and the like, showing how to remove the top of this cup and glue it on the top of another, and so on, or glue it to the bottom of the machine reader itself and just insert any cup you want.[9]

In reality, he said, Keurig could have done more with the 2.0 from the standpoint of interactivity and keeping out competition.[10] But many consumers did not see it that way and neither did some other coffee purveyors, as we see later.

The Secret to Keurig's Success

Keurig's success, according to Van Winkle, all starts with the consumer solution. He stressed that it was a no-brainer. A large portion of the US population drinks coffee. Coffee is very important to them. "Coffee is brewed at home," he said, "this isn't like a SodaStream where I'm going to make soda at home or I can buy it in a can. I can't buy hot coffee at the grocery store and drink it every two weeks. I have to make it at home."

Everyone who makes coffee needs an appliance. That meant that a new coffee brewer would be replacing a machine that somebody already had. "I think the last time I saw the numbers," Van Winkle said, "there were ninety million homes with a coffee maker, and there were twenty million coffee makers sold a year. So basically the math is every four and a half years somebody's throwing away their coffee maker and buying a new one."

So, there was a replacement cycle the brewer maker had to sell into. Everybody likely already had some kind of machine or equipment to make coffee. A coffeemaker was an essential appliance that was used every day at least once a day. The coffeemaker was not like a big bulky food processor or stand mixer that would take up precious real estate on the kitchen counter. A new coffee brewer would replace something that was already being heavily used.[11] And the Keurig, summed up Van Winkle, "was dramatically more convenient."

The Keurig had a lot of advantages and it was a solution for a lot of people. The time saving and the accessibility really made a difference. Van Winkle observed that while a lot of people might set their drip coffeemaker to start brewing at a certain time in the morning, most don't.[12] "Being able to make a cup of coffee in thirty to forty seconds was a significant improvement," he said. "The brands benefited in the long run because there was more sampling. Rather than buying a pound of coffee, you could buy eight cups at a time." More coffee drinkers got to experience an increasing number of brands.

For instance, now Twinings of London, the venerable three hundred-year-old tea company, offers coffee in K-Cups (in addition to tea K-Cups, of course). Starbucks also joined Keurig and, after parting ways with Tassimo, Lavazza, an Italian coffee brand, is also available in K-Cups.

In addition to the brand selection, the business model that Keurig deployed allowed them to be successful. Normally, when you try and create an entire new consumer product it can be very expensive. "The model that Keurig started and then Green Mountain continued after they acquired

Keurig was really not to have to deploy any capital into the manufacturing of the machines. They outsource the manufacturing to suppliers in China. You obviously have to carry inventory. But you really weren't deploying any capital against building the machines . . ." They didn't have to make money on the machines, so they could sell them at a price point where they delivered a very attractive and quality product at a price that was appealing to consumers.[13]

The big advantage Keurig had over its competition was that the manufacturers of competing machines had to make a profit on the machine.[14] With household appliances, reasoned Van Winkle, usually the heavier they are, the more expensive they are. "A really inexpensive plastic coffee maker you can pick up at Walmart for ten dollars is a lot different than a Cuisinart Grind & Brew that you pick up at Bed, Bath, & Beyond for one hundred and fifty dollars. So the model allowed them to get a good price point with a good quality machine which allowed them to build their household penetration."

By initially using third-party partners, brands that were going to spend their own money to build manufacturing, Keurig avoided needing to make back their money on the brewers. "Now, ultimately," Van Winkle said, "Green Mountain acquire[d] all of the licensees, acquire[d] Keurig, when they [were] the ones putting all the capital behind K-Cup manufacturing facilities and K-Cup manufacturing equipment, but the initial Keurig model was almost an outsourced model in all respects except for marketing and R & D." Keurig used a good business model with a good consumer solution and that is what made it.[15] It eventually became very obvious that the quality of the coffee coming out of the Keurig K-Cup machines was as good as you were getting elsewhere. And you could brew it right there in your kitchen in a matter of seconds.

The Emergence or Escalation of Other Single-Serve Brands

Keurig and the K-Cup may be the most well-known, especially in the United States, but what about the other single-serve coffee options mentioned before? Although its burgeoning growth of the past decades has slowed,[16] Nespresso is still the leading brand in Europe, as of this writing, and has been making inroads in the United States and Canada. In 2014, Nespresso introduced their VertuoLine System, specifically designed to cater to the American preferences, as Nespresso says on their website:[17]

> VertuoLine system [is] the first *Nespresso* machine that brews both American style large-cup coffee and authentic espresso. Launched exclusively in the US and Canada, *VertuoLine* directly appeals to large-cup coffee preference in North America. In the same way that it pioneered the premium portioned coffee segment in Europe more than 25 years ago, *Nespresso* aims to revolutionize the large-cup coffee segment in North America.[18]

Nespresso has figured out how to charm the serious single-serve coffee lover. In 2006, George Clooney became the spokesperson for Nespresso and appeared in ads for the high-end espresso machine. Some of those ads also featured Danny DeVito and John Malkovich. However, the ads didn't appear in the United States until 2015.

The single-serve market is getting somewhat crowded and each brand wants to capture coffee drinkers who crave the single-serve option. In the United States, Keurig has about an 85 percent share of the single-serve capsule market and Nespresso, with the launch of its VertuoLine, is hoping to garner more than the 4 percent share of the US coffee capsule market it had as of 2013.[19] It is a safe bet that since JAB's takeover of Keurig, that brand will be looking at increasing its market share in Europe. JAB already has the biggest piece of the coffee capsule market on the planet, and that is where the growth and the money are.[20] Senseo, the single-serve brewer that uses coffee pods that contain no plastic, using little coffee-filled pillows, has been and is more popular in Europe than it is stateside, with a 10 percent global share of the single-serve market, just behind Nespresso with an 11 percent global market share, as of 2013.[21, 22]

Nestlé released its Nescafe Dolce Gusto in 2006 in Europe, which is a more modestly priced alternative to its Nespresso. While some see this as Nestlé challenging itself,[23] it seems like a smart way to hedge its bets in the single-serve marketplace. While Nestlé's Nespresso's European market share has fallen from 2010 to 2015, Nestlé's Dolce Gusto has risen in that time period.

Tassimo joined the caffeine fray in 2004 in France. Like other single-serve coffee companies, Tassimo was involved in multiple changing coffee-partner scenarios over the years. Ethical Coffee Company came into being in 2008 under the guidance of Nestlé's Nespresso's former boss, Jean Paul Gaillard. Ethical, as its name might imply, uses biodegradable pods.

With single-serve coffee, there is no "Can't we all just get along?" Keeping up with who owns what can be very confusing and requires lots of . . . coffee. Which leads to disagreements.

CHAPTER 8

Turf Wars: Keep Your
Pod Out of My Brewer

It's just a bit of coffee in a little pod that goes into a brewer, so how many different ways can this be done? Apparently, many. Hence, skirmishes aplenty. The coffee pods that work in one brewer will often not work in another. And, depending upon the point of view, that's just fine. Or not.

It takes years of research, development, and money to make a new product, so can you blame a company for trying to hold onto all of the profits for as long as it can? After all, as with any new product, it is the original company that spends the time and resources to come up with the idea. As with pharmaceutical research, the ability to keep the profits to themselves through patents for several years makes the research pay off. Then other companies can follow and improve on or change the idea of the original. The original company then figures out a way to turn things back around by producing a slightly different design of the brewer or a host of different types of pods. Problems can arise, though, when a company changes the design of its brewer to ensure that only its own pods will work in their brewers. And there is, of course, the matter of patent infringement.

Of course, the maker of a particular coffee brewer, say, Company A, would want consumers to buy the pods made by Company A to use in Company A's brewer. That is where most of the profits in single serve are. But consumers want to make their own choices. And Company B would want its coffee pods or capsules to be compatible in Company A's brewer as well as Company B's, or Company C's, and so on.

Things can get very dicey when patents expire or are about to, so it stands to reason that a company would want to make as much profit as it can before its designs, mechanicals, and processes are no longer proprietary.

Since Nespresso and Keurig are the biggest players in the single-serve market in their respective main marketplaces, it is not surprising that these two companies have had to stand up for their products more than a few times. Here are just some of the examples of single-serve coffee brouhaha:

January 2007—Keurig filed a patent infringement lawsuit against Kraft that alleged Kraft's Tassimo T-Discs infringed on one of Keurig's patents. Both parties agreed on a settlement in 2008.[1, 2]

2011—The Rogers Family Company's Rogers Family Coffee came out with its OneCup single-serve coffee pod that is compatible with the Keurig. Keurig sued the Rogers Family Company for design patent infringement.[3]

2011—Sturm Foods, a subsidiary of Treehouse Foods, got into trouble for selling their Grove Square Coffee pods that contained mostly instant or freeze-dried coffee. The Grove Square Coffee pod looked like a K-Cup but there was no filter inside the cup. Keurig still had a patent for the design of the filter inside the K-Cup, but Sturm Foods came out with their version of the K-Cup before Keurig's patent expired. The suit snowballed into a class action that was revived over the years and involved people from at least eight states.[4, 5, 6, 7]

2012—Coffee drinkers take their coffee very seriously. A lot of people bought Kraft's Tassimo single-serve brewers because they loved that Starbucks coffee was available in Tassimo T-Discs and they could brew their beloved Starbucks at home. These folks were pretty angry when Starbucks was no longer available in the Tassimo Brewer's T-Discs, and Keurig began offering Starbucks in their K-Cups instead (the two systems are not compatible).[8, 9] A class action false advertising lawsuit was filed against both Kraft and Starbucks for allegedly continuing to promise Tassimo coffee brewing system buyers that Starbucks cups would be available when Starbucks moved over to the Keurig system.[10, 11] The suit, however, was denied certification[12] in 2014 and was dismissed in 2016. Still, it shows you how intense coffee drinkers are about their coffee.[13]

2013—Judge rules the Rogers Family Company did not infringe on Keurig's patent.[14]

February 2014—Keurig is sued by Treehouse Foods over the Keurig 2.0 brewer.[15, 16, 17] Treehouse Foods maintained that Keurig was trying to monopolize the single-serve coffee market.

March 12, 2014—The United States Court of Appeals confirmed a previous decision that found that the Rogers Family Company's OneCup single-serve coffee pod did not infringe on Keurig's patents.[18]

March 13, 2014—The Rogers Family Company sues Keurig for violations of federal antitrust as well as for unfair competition.[19]

April 2014—Continuing in the vein started by the Rogers Family Company and Treehouse Foods, twelve class action complaints from people in four states and a Maryland insurance company were launched against Keurig for violating antitrust laws because the Keurig 2.0 brewer, which would be launched later that year, would accept only Keurig K-Cups.[20, 21]

April 2014—As a result of a probe by the French Competition Authority for unfairly discouraging the use of competitors' espresso capsules in Nespresso's brewers,[22, 23] Nespresso acquiesced to concerns and agreed to let rival coffeemakers produce capsules that can be used in Nespresso's brewers. Nespresso had changed the design of its brewer or capsules too often and too close to when a competitor was introducing a brewer, according to the complaint. This commitment of Nespresso to the French authority to resolve the competition issue is considered groundbreaking because in that commitment Nespresso agreed, among other things, to give competitors technical details about its new brewers four months in advance to Nespresso's marketing the machines. Nespresso also agreed to make available to rivals the fifteen latest prototypes of new brewers so that these other companies would be able to conduct compatibility tests with their capsules. Nespresso also agreed to let the French authority know the reasons for any technical adjustments far ahead of manufacturing the new designs. This was seen as something for other companies to watch since these kinds of commitments would seem to frustrate the whole idea behind innovation.[24, 25]

May 2014—Nespresso, USA, sues HiLine Coffee Company for trademark infringement, among other things, and for violating unfair competition laws.[26, 27] HiLine Coffee, based in New York, said its goal was offering customers quality coffee at an affordable price. HiLine Coffee had launched in July of 2013 and urged consumers to declare "Independence from Nespresso."[28] This did not please Nespresso.

August 2014—Keurig introduces the 2.0 brewer that will accept only Keurig K-Cups.

November 2014—Rogers Family Company comes out with the Roger's Freedom Clip, which can circumvent the technology of Keurig's new 2.0 brewer that allows only K-Cups authorized by Keurig, which have a code that the 2.0 brewer recognizes.[29, 30, 31]

January 2015—Ethical Coffee Company (owned by a former Nestlé chief executive) lodges a complaint[32] in a Paris court against Nespresso saying that a new part in Nespresso's brewer prevented Ethical's coffee capsules from being used in the Nespresso brewer. Nespresso's patent for this part in its brewer was declared void.[33, 34]

January, 2016—Nespresso sues Israeli company Espresso Club for featuring a very George Clooney-esque actor in their ads.[35, 36] While at the start of the ad there is a warning that the actor is not George Clooney, there are enough similarities to Nespresso's ads[37] that have featured Clooney in its advertising since 2006 that Nespresso took offense.

PART THREE

COFFEE FOR ONE EVOLVES

CHAPTER 9

The Single-Serve Environmental Quandary and Some Alternatives

I n the coffee brewing industry, as in everything else, there is a reaction for every action and there have been countless reactions to each twist and turn in the single-serve industry. Some companies are fighting back with alternatives that pressed-for-time people can use with a clearer environmental conscious.

Rogers Family Company

John W. "JR" Rogers, vice president of Lincoln, California's, Rogers Family Company, is one of the four adult children of company founders Jon B. Rogers and Barbara Rogers. All four children work full time at the company, so it really is a family operation. As JR tells it, the company, formed in 1986, initially had no intentions of going into the single-serve coffee business. He had seen single-serve coffee brewers at gas stations, car washes, and other places around town. But he didn't think much of it at first: "We had no interest in getting into the single serve at all when it first came out. I didn't even think it was that particularly a great way to make coffee . . ." He thought that the single-serve brewer would be like, as he said, the bread maker in the '80s: "Bread makers were really hot, and there was one in every darn house. Everyone was baking bread for about eight months, and then it just died off."[1]

But the single-serve brewer was not like the bread maker. As single-serve coffee got bigger and bigger, he realized they had to be a part of it, but they wanted to accomplish three things. "One," JR said, "if we were going to do it, we wanted to make it taste better, [two], we wanted to reduce the environmental footprint, and [three], we wanted it to be cheaper because it was pretty expensive. We thought if we could accomplish those three goals that we could be successful. It wasn't a 'let's make the biodegradable single-serve cup.' It really was three phases of the whole thing." Their first version of the single-serve coffee pod took about two years to develop and came out in 2011.

Rogers Family had the help of one of their equipment manufacturers in creating the coffee pods. They reduced the packing cost by 30 percent by using less plastic. Their company as a whole uses less plastic, he pointed out. "We started working on the idea of, okay, can we improve on this?" he said. "It led to the 100 percent compostable cup . . ." It took a lot of time and testing to be certified biodegradable, but they did it. All the components have been certified biodegradable and are made from plant-based renewable resources.

Rogers Family, whose brands include San Francisco Bay Coffee and the Organic Coffee Company, oversees the coffee production from start to finish. With their OneCup, Rogers went after Keurig one biodegradable single serve at a time. In 2014, they came out with an ingenious invention called the Freedom Clip, to help consumers bypass the proprietary barricade that Keurig had built into its 2.0 brewer that would permit only K-Cups to be used in the machine.

Rogers Family got the idea for the Freedom Clip when they started to hear rumblings that Keurig was coming out with the new machine that was going to be proprietary and work only with that company's K-Cups.[2, 3] Rogers wanted to find out about the new brewer's limitations but they were not into industrial espionage.

"We were having a lot of trouble getting our product in the marketplace because of this new machine," JR said of the Keurig 2.0. "Our stuff [wouldn't] work with it, no one else's [would], it [was] going to have to be Keurig-approved, so there was a whole big flurry and scurry in the marketplace."[4, 5]

So the people at Rogers did what any forward-thinking, smart company would do. "Once the machine came out, we bought one," JR said. "We'd figured how to make something else work in it. We certainly couldn't come out and change our products right away because we had inventories of packaging material and things." They needed to figure out how to make things work using what they already had. They did figure out a way to make it work and how to make any brand of K-Cup-like coffee pods compatible with the 2.0 brewer. They invented the Freedom Clip. And they gave it away for free.

The design of the Freedom Clip tricked the Keurig 2.0 into thinking the unauthorized pod, like ones from Rogers, were approved pods. The machine could then brew coffee using pods other than K-Cups. The clip attached to the inside of the machine, fooling the brewer into "thinking" that the coffee pod was an authorized product, so the machine would work. The Freedom Clip, as JR said, "Certainly helped other people's products, too, but what it did was it opened up competition in the marketplace."

The Next Wave for Single Serve

JR said that the next wave for single-serve coffee is to be environmentally friendly. "People are looking at what they're doing every morning," he stressed, "and they open up their trash can, they see fifteen plastic cups there which are going to go into the landfill, and they're never going to go away. Every piece of plastic that's ever been made since the beginning of time is still here in some format. It just doesn't go away, so I think people are seeing that, and wondering if they really want to continue doing that to the planet."

The Rogers Family Company were not alone in this thinking and they are not alone in doing something about it.

For instance, there are musicians. Musicians and coffee go together like music and lyrics. Some famous musicians have had affiliations with certain coffee roasters and chose blends that they liked. That brew was promoted in tandem with the release of a new album. Intelligentsia Coffee, for instance, has worked with St. Vincent, The New Pornographers, and Wilco. They invite the musicians in, they sample the coffees, select a coffee, and then they have a collaboration for an album launch.

Other musicians love coffee so much they started their own coffee companies. Aerosmith's Joey Kramer's Rockin' & Roastin', for example, and Green Day's Oakland Coffee Works.

Green Day and Oakland Coffee Works

Rogers Family Company partnered with Oakland Coffee Works, started and owned by Green Day members Mike Dirnt and Billie Joe Armstrong. Not only does Oakland Coffee Works sell its coffee in bags made from certified compostable materials (even the valve in the bag is biodegradable), but they also offer single-serve pods made from compostables. As Oakland Coffee Works announced in a statement, "First there was diner coffee, then there was second wave coffee, like Starbucks, and then came the third wave with artisanal coffee—but this is the next step: organic, truly high-quality coffee that fairly supports the farmers who grow it and that comes in packaging made from fully compostable materials."

The Green Day musicians came up with an idea for a business that would not only offer great coffee, but that would make a difference with the environment. They are very committed to this next stage of single-serve coffee, as evidenced by an email exchange we had: "We are ushering in the Fourth Wave of premium coffee, which values environmental sustainability and a personal connection to the farmers, in addition to the passion for quality coffee and focus on origin that defined the Third Wave. We hope that other companies will follow our lead and transition to more sustainable and affordable options. It will not be easy, but we hope that the future will be free of single-use plastic pods and bags."[6]

As Mike Dirnt of Green Day said of the single-serve option for coffee, "We know that a majority of people use single-serve cups and that the problem of single-use plastic will not go away unless a viable solution is presented. Compostable pods are a great solution. That being said, as a parent of three, I also understand the need for a cup of coffee immediately."

There was never any doubt about what kind of business the musicians would get involved in. They'd been seriously into coffee for more than a decade. Oakland Coffee Works just seemed like the obvious venture. "We're crazy about coffee," the musicians stated. "We love it. We have been sourcing our own beans and making our own blends for more than ten years. A few years ago, we thought it was ready to share with the community. However, we didn't want to add to the sea of trash. We looked around for 100 percent compostable packaging and we found that it didn't exist . . . yet. That led us on the road to where we are now. In this quest we have met a lot of really cool, like-minded people who have helped us along the way. It's been a great journey!"

Coffee it was, and had to be, but coffee done with global responsibility in mind. "Every day, millions of people drink (at least!) a cup of coffee. It's one of the largest traded commodities in the world," said the rockers. "We chose to follow our passion for coffee through by showing that you don't have to compromise great taste and affordability for sustainability. This is organic coffee that is easy to drink, at an affordable price, and down-right delicious. All the while, it is supporting farmers through fair wages, investment in community infrastructure, and reduction of harmful chemicals in the environment. Throw compostable packaging into the mix and you have a product that is unapologetically sustainable. How could we not get into the coffee game when we knew we could accomplish that?"

And in some small way being in the music business prepared them for the coffee business. Said Dirnt: "I have served many cups of coffee as a teen working in restaurants. I consider myself a barista of sorts backstage at every show on tour. I've also enjoyed the pleasure of visiting some of the very best, artisanal coffee houses in the world."

Armstrong and Dirnt partnered with Rogers Family because, as they said, "Until now, no one had found a way to make coffee packaging completely compostable. Everyone told us it couldn't be done, but we wouldn't take 'no' for an answer. On our journey to compostable solutions, we met ingenious engineers and forward-thinkers, including the like-minded revolutionaries over at SF Bay Coffee, who were seeking to make their OneCup pods fully compostable. We decided to work together to pool resources and maximize the opportunity for success in finding a viable compostable option. It hasn't been an easy journey, but it's been worth it."

Finding the right coffee was done very carefully. They all sat around the cupping tables, to taste and test, and just cupped, and cupped, and cupped, and created some special blends from some smaller estates that Rogers buys coffee from. Rogers has a great many farms around the world where they buy the entire crop. "We created some custom blends for them, and then went out with all the environmentally friendly packaging, and we're trying to sell it to the stores of America," JR of Rogers Family said.

It wasn't easy getting everything just right. According to the folks of Oakland Coffee Works: "You can't let perfection get in the way of progress. We believe that you always need to be striving to produce the most sustainable, well-made products. That means putting our best products out there and continually working to perfect them. Any step in the right direction gets the ball rolling on combatting plastic waste. Our current packaging is just the first step in this revolution."

Rogers Family and Oakland Coffee Works are a good fit. "We do a whole lot of things other than just this [coffee]," JR said. "They [Oakland Coffee] were thinking along the lines of doing the same sort of stuff, making a difference, and that sort of thing, so we just started talking . . ." At first, JR said Rogers Family wasn't so interested. They tended to do their own thing and weren't sure about having partners. Over the years they have been approached by chefs and the like to get involved with co-branding, but they always said, "no thanks." But, the guys at Oakland Coffee Works were very convincing. As JR put it, it was, "'Just come and sit down, and let's talk.' They were very passionate. They're very smart. It was clear that they wanted to do the same sort of things that we were doing, and they [could] reach a group of people that we really [couldn't] reach, like who they are. We knew that we could all do some really great things together, and that's what we've started doing."

And the thirst for the single cup will just keep growing. "It's a fraction of what's out there." Still, there is a lot of competition around these days and it is not easy to compete in the marketplace with, as JR put it, "the eight-hundred-pound gorilla sitting on everybody's chest." The different types of brewers in the mix add to the confusion. "The Keurig machine is the one that's used in America," Rogers observed, "and I think the latest numbers are somewhere between about 25 percent to 30 percent of the households, but it's over 50 percent of the coffee market dollars right now. We're seeing from the numbers there's a lot more competition out there." There are also a lot more special deals and promotions at the retail level.

Added JR, "The consumer is winning because of the competition. The price has gone down. I believe so. We're just thinking that the next phase to keep it, if the category wants to grow, it is going to have to be through an environmentally friendly one."

No doubt that even with sales and promotion, the cost of a cup of coffee made with the single-serve brewer is a lot higher that a cup of coffee using a coffee pot. "When you get right down to it," JR said, "it's cheaper for you to make a pot of coffee, pour one cup, and pour the rest down the drain. Our whole goal with the thing is to just make this so that it'll go in your green bin with your leaves, and your lawn clippings, and all that sort of stuff . . ." After a period of time ". . . it turns into dirt, so it will actually help the planet."

Other companies are following the path to more environmentally friendly single-serve coffee options. Hills Bros. Coffee launched the Massimo Zanetti Beverage brand that uses BPI certified 100 percent compostable coffee pods—the PURPOD100™—in 2016. Massimo is one of the largest coffee roasters with nationally known retail brands such as

Chock full o'Nuts, Chase & Sanborn, and others, in addition to Hills Bros.

K-Cup and Recycling

Single-serve coffee and other portion-pack beverages save time, to be sure. But, depending upon several factors, the real cost of single serve may not translate into just time versus money. The pileup of plastic has been getting the attention it deserves. Can convenience exist in good conscience? How much plastic is too much? More than nine billion K-Cups were sold in 2015. Is recycling a viable option?

Keurig sees the recyclable K-Cup as the next breakthrough and they have been working toward that end for a number of years. Keurig's chief sustainability officer Monique Oxender is in charge of Keurig's work with Brewing a Better World. On their website, Keurig points out that a lot of waste is on the manufacturing side and they have worked toward lessening that impact.[7]

With the Keurig Vue brewer that was introduced in 2012, the company was able to offer more environmentally friendly coffee pods, which are made of recyclable #5 plastic. These were slightly smaller versions of the K-Cups. With the coffee pods for the Vue, consumers could just peel off the top, throw away the "inside" (the pouch, coffee filter, coffee, and the top) and recycle the plastic. Keurig introduced its My K-Cup reusable coffee filter for its brewers in 2005.

It appears that the environmental controversy hasn't really had a significant impact on Keurig's long-term success, and the recycling issues didn't seem to be that much of an impediment. Does it keep some consumers away? Some, yes.

The single-serve option has been steeped in controversy for years. Hamburg, Germany, made news in 2015 when the city banned single-serve coffee pods from government buildings. There are those who are vehemently against single serve, particularly in its manifestation as plastic pod. There's even a website, Kill The K-Cup, devoted to, well, killing the K-Cup.[8]

At present, Keurig has several K-Cups that are recyclable, including Breakfast Blend, Nantucket Blend, and Hazelnut.[9] Keurig has announced plans to produce 100 percent of K-Cup pods in Canada in a recyclable format by the end of 2018. Keurig also stated on their website that they are on track to have 100 percent of K-Cup pods recyclable by the end of 2020.

Keurig states on their site that they want their pods to be effectively recycled and they are working with recyclers and industry experts to improve the capture rate of valuable small plastic items, such as their pods.[10] They are using polypropylene #5 plastic in their recyclable K-Cup pods and maintain on their website that polypropylene #5 plastic performs well in their brewing system, is accepted for recycling in a majority of communities in the United States and Canada, and is in high demand as a recovered material.[11]

Keurig says it has tested the new recyclable in "real world recycling and recovery facilities." The consumer just has to "peel the foil lid. Empty the used coffee grounds. Place the empty pod in the recycling bin." Keurig is "transitioning over 100 manufacturing lines across eight North American production facilities to manufacture recyclable K-Cup pods for all Keurig brands."[12] While they are currently focused on recyclability, Keurig is exploring the use of many different materials, including those that are compostable.

An increasing number of coffee drinkers are realizing that compostable, or at least recyclable, pods are the way to go. According to the Global Food & Drink Trends Survey released by Mintel, a global marketing intelligence agency, 40 percent of Canadian adults who drink coffee and/or tea agree that single-serve coffee or tea pods should be compostable or biodegradable.[13]

CHAPTER 10

Giving Back

Laughing Man Coffee is well-known because of the efforts of actor Hugh Jackman, its cofounder. As Jackman said in a press release, "We started Laughing Man Coffee and Tea to fulfill a commitment I made to share the amazing products and story of an Ethiopian coffee farmer named Dukale. Six years later, it's humbling to think that, through this agreement, Dukale's exceptional coffee will be enjoyed by millions through the convenience of the Keurig brewing system."

Hugh Jackman started Laughing Man Coffee Foundation in 2011 to offer farmers in developing countries a marketplace to sell their coffee to US coffee lovers. Jackman contributes 100 percent of the profits to the Laughing Man Foundation, which supports educational programs, community development, and entrepreneurship worldwide.

David Steingard is a cofounder of Laughing Man Coffee and is the CEO of the coffee company and the director of the Laughing Man Foundation. How did Steingard, a former assistant district attorney of Kings County in New York become a part of this venture with Jackman?

According to Steingard, it all happened pretty organically. "It was," he said in an interview, "sort of two different unknown paths coming together. We had been family friends for a while, and I'm a lawyer. I was a criminal prosecutor before I got into coffee, and he was global ambassador for an NGO [non-government organization] called World Vision Australia." World Vision provides economic confidence-building throughout the world on a community basis. Jackman has been a longtime supporter of a number of area development programs, and in 2009 he and his wife, actress and producer Deborra-Lee Furness, took a trip to Ethiopia to see how World Vision's work empowered communities at ground level and to make a documentary about World Vision's work there. They met Dukale and his family, and saw their coffee plantation.[1]

Steingard thinks that this trip and meeting Dukale was a bit of a defining moment for Jackman, the coming together of a lot of different things that he had read about and had done. Jackman "is heavily philanthropic, and really well-read in this field, and different areas of micro-finance, and so I think for him it was sort of an 'Aha' moment." Jackman met Dukale, and he promised him he would help. "I don't think he even knew what that meant, but he was really moved."

David Steingard is no stranger to coffee. His family has been in the coffee business since the 1970s, before coffee became a phenomenon unto itself, in the form of the Cupping Room Café, a neighborhood place where locals and the well-known alike gather. The name of the New York City establishment refers to its beginnings as a wholesale coffee supplier where various blends of coffee were brewed and tasted—cupping—by prospective buyers. Steingard wanted to leave law and get back into the coffee business. As he said, "There were a lot of great things happening that I was interested in, as far as the specialty coffee movement, and the sort of socioeconomic issues built into it, such as the consumer getting more interested in the farmers." He liked what was happening and that it dovetailed nicely with the idea of business entrepreneurship.

One day when Steingard and Jackman were talking, Steingard randomly mentioned getting back into coffee, and Jackman asked if he wanted a partner. Steingard said, "Well, that'd be amazing, but let's do something like Paul Newman." [The Paul Newman model is that all profits go to charity.] Said Steingard, "We all really love his story, and I sort of consider Hugh the sort of Paul Newman 2.0, really well respected, known to be philanthropic, very nice, so I thought it'd be something that we could do."

The idea was that the café would support the foundation, and as they continued to grow, the foundation would give back to farmers. Currently, the majority of their effort goes back to Dukale, whether it be equipment, or scholarships, or things like that.

Jackman spoke at the United Nations in 2009 and told Dukale's story during Climate Change Week. The documentary film *Dukale's Dream* came out that year and has been recut a number of times. "What has been so nice about the whole journey of the coffee company has been it has been really organic," Steingard said. "It hasn't been planned out much. It's just been sort of following events. When we opened the café, we then recut the film to show again the birth of this café inspired by this real person, Dukale, and bringing his coffee over and trying to share it with the world, and him not being the only person in the world, but sort of our muse, if you will, because he's certainly not the only farmer in that situation."

When they were approached by Green Mountain, the film was recut again to reiterate the message of meeting this farmer, to growing the company and going national. The message and great mission were a very powerful story.

By the way, although this is not widely known, the origin of the name Laughing Man stems from the fact that both Jackman and Steingard are big J. D. Salinger fans, and the name comes from the title of a short story that Salinger wrote that appeared in *The New Yorker* in 1949. But the name also is a great way to demonstrate an idea or ethos of unity, Steingard said. Thinking about best friends laughing together, breaking down barriers, having a sense of commonality no matter who you are. "Even if you're a stranger, if you get into that moment of great laughter, you have this moment of unity, and hope, and this sense that those who are able to laugh freely are those who have the ability to provide for themselves, create their own destiny, have work, have fulfillment, and this was something that we hoped the foundation can help provide," Steingard said.

One of the things in the coffee industry that has improved is that there has been a lot of talk and a good amount of action around fair trade. The term "fair trade" is sometimes used as an umbrella term for a sustainable supply chain. "Obviously," said Steingard, "[World] Fair Trade Organization does a specific thing. What I think is good about the [World] Fair Trade Organization, but as well as all the other certifications, is it just begins to keep raising the bar on transparency, and quality coffee, and a sustainable living for the people producing it." Fair trade and all that it stands for is, of course, essential. Steingard believes that it ideally should be made more clear to more people that fair trade also leads to a better cup of coffee. "If everybody plays their part really well, and invests in each other," he added, "you end up with a better product. I think that's important."

And there is always room for improvement. Coffee, he said, generally comes from some very unstable areas so more can be done to have increasing transparency where possible at the supply chain level.

On the retail side, there has been a lot of improvement and a little more openness from the specialty coffee movement, Steingard found. Not only is there great customer service, there are efforts to educate and introduce people to specialty coffee and to the idea that paying a little more for coffee that is organic- or fair-trade or rain-forest certified, or whatever the certification is, again leads to a better experience for the end consumer.

Steingard thinks that this is happening more in food than in other industries, maybe because with food it is more immediate. While there has been a lot of good work done, you can always refine how you tell the story and how you educate, and how you welcome people into this movement.

The vision of Laughing Man Worldwide is basically focused on making Laughing Man Coffee a success, and the foundation in the future will look to support entrepreneurs, as well as give back to the farmer where it can, but right now mostly the focus is on the coffee.

Steingard says that the foundation in a way is in its infancy, because its funding and growth come from the growth of the Laughing Man coffee shop (as of this writing, there are two in NYC) and it has, of course, taken some years to make that sustainable. "I think right now we're in this exciting time of trying to go deeper and clarify the things that we are interested in," he said. "We've always worked with World Vision. We've always remained connected to Dukale and the Kochere region, and giving back there. I think certainly this year and [in] the coming years, you'll see greater depth of projects and clarification, especially with the partnership with Keurig Green Mountain."

Green Day also gives back through Fueled by Love, a charitable organization committed to delivering funding and infrastructure at the local level to support communities in the regions where coffee is produced.[2] They work with Crescendos Alliance, which is a nonprofit organization that works to *better the quality of life in remote, rural settings.* Some projects they have worked on together are supporting a new clinic in a region in Peru that had no emergency medical service, expert water testing to assess the integrity of a village's water supply, starting a local learning center to help with the community's childhood educational resources, and starting programs to offer youth counseling in the area.[3, 4]

They are very committed to this, as they emphasized in our interview, "We will continue to forge deeper partnerships with the farmers and communities that grow our coffee beans. We will also be creating an arm of Fueled By Love that will focus on helping other like-minded companies through the process of incorporating fully compostable packaging."[5]

The Rogers Family Company is also dedicated to being socially and environmentally responsible. Through sales of their products, the Rogers family has improved housing, medical access, water quality, environment, and more in the areas where coffee is grown, including Mexico, Indonesia, Central America, and Rwanda.

In addition to making an environmentally friendly single serve, Rogers Family Company has built seventy schools around the world and has provided housing for thousands of workers. As outlined on their website,

Rogers Family has a Community Aid program that is based on three principles:

1. Care for Farmers: Long-term contracts so coffee framers can be fair to their employees and earn a reasonable profit for their hard work, keeping in mind the costs of production, infrastructure, and maintenance.

2. Care for the Community: Rogers Family's investment in the Community Aid program runs about $1,000,000 a year, which goes to education, nutrition, and health-care programs that help break the cycle of poverty in their partner coffee growing communities. From 2001 to 2009, they constructed twenty-five schools, 140 bathrooms, 130 housing units, fifteen clinics, and sixty kitchens in communities throughout Central America, South America, Rwanda, and Southeast Asia (Sumatra and Papua New Guinea).

3. Care for the Environment: Rogers Family supports sustainable, responsible farming. This means shade-grown, organic coffee, and farmlands with substantial areas left in their natural state so that the ecosystem can continue to thrive. Responsible farming not only means excellent coffee, but it also helps keep the land, people, and wildlife healthy everywhere their coffee is grown. They use natural, sustainable methods, such as using ten billion worms to turn coffee farm waste into five thousand pounds of pure fertilizer each week.[6]

Rogers Family also is adamant about paying a fair price for the coffee. Said JR, "We pay about a dollar more than the market is right now. We're paying about $2.37 a pound for coffee when everybody else is paying a buck thirty, or a buck fifty."[7]

CHAPTER 11

Coffee and Health

Drink More—It's Good for You!

Like quite a few other foods and beverages (eggs, butter, wine), it seems as if one year coffee is extolled for its health benefits and the next year it is vilified as an impediment to a healthy lifestyle. The caffeine in coffee can be very beneficial and not only for the obvious reason of brightening the coffee drinker's outlook and increasing energy levels.[1] The caffeine in coffee might have health benefits, as well. [Of course, how much caffeine is too much can vary from person to person, and checking with your doctor or other medical or health professional about your diet—or changing your diet—is important. This book is not recommending anything, just reporting on recent studies.] Coffee is rich in magnesium, niacin, and potassium, and contains powerful compounds like chlorogenic acid and polyphenols, which are formidable antioxidants that can help thwart damage to cells. That is good news, indeed.

According to the American Cancer Society, coffee beans are chock full of antioxidants that might protect against cancer.[2] Earlier studies had been mixed about this added benefit of the bean, but larger and more precise studies have found that coffee might indeed protect against some cancers, including prostate, liver, endometrial, and some mouth and throat.

Coffee may reduce the risk of gallstones and inhibit the occurrence of colon cancer.[3]

True, the benefits kicked in when the participants in the studies drank more than four cups and up to six cups of coffee per day. Some people would say that is a great deal of coffee. Others, though, think of it as just eighteen hours' worth of enjoyable coffee drinking. And drinking lots of coffee alone is no guarantee against cancer. You have to lead an otherwise healthy lifestyle as well.

Dr. Marilyn Cornelis, a nutritionist at the Northwestern University Feinberg School of Medicine, said that the coffee-cancer connection can vary by cancer. With some cancers, the links are much stronger and more consistent. For other cancers, the link is not as consistent.[4]

Researchers at Harvard have been studying the benefits of coffee for years.[5] In 2014, the international research team, led by Dr. Cornelis who was a research associate at the Harvard T. H. Chan School of Public Health at the time, discovered six new human genes that interact with coffee.[6] Only two human genes had previously been linked with interacting with coffee. Studies have found that coffee can help ward off type 2 diabetes and cardiovascular disease, and researchers are looking closely at whether coffee can keep Parkinson's disease at bay. Coffee might even help prevent dental cavities. Coffee also has a possible role in the mitigation or prevention of some other conditions or diseases including migraines, cardiovascular disease, depression, and dementia.

Type 2 Diabetes

Studies have shown that drinking coffee may help reduce the risk of getting type 2 diabetes in the first place.[7] But what if you already have type 2 diabetes?[8, 9] Isn't caffeine a problem when managing this disease and diet? Dr. Cornelis found that it might not be the caffeine in coffee that has the benefits to help foil some diseases. In fact, caffeine has been proven to raise glucose levels in some cases. So, what is behind the beneficial side of coffee? Dr. Cornelis wondered if there were chemical compounds in coffee other than caffeine that provided health benefits, like the high antioxidants. The delicious fragrance of coffee is actually the result of the plethora of chemical compounds that could be the secret to the powers of the bean. There is much we do not know about how the chemical compounds found in coffee interact with the body. Dr. Cornelis is researching what the chemical compounds are and how they affect the body. She is exploring a study in Finland, a country where people drink on average more coffee per capita than anywhere else in the world, 2.64 cups per day.[10]

Dr. Cornelis pointed out that there is a lot of interest in how coffee can affect our health and there is quite a bit of research around the specifics: "It probably varies by the type of health outcomes you're looking at," she said. Most of this is based on either experimental data or epidemiological data—studies of large populations over time.

There are certain diseases or conditions that coffee does seem to affect in a favorable way. "For certain health outcomes that impact the brain such as Alzheimer's disease or other neurological disorders like Parkinson's," stated Dr. Cornelis, "there's some evidence and a general strong hypothesis suggesting that it's the caffeine component of coffee, but for other outcomes—diabetes is probably one of the better examples—it could be other things in coffee. For example, the polyphenols, more specifically the chlorogenic acid." Chlorogenic acid occurs naturally in plants, and is an important part of their metabolic functions.[11]

Chlorogenic acid can be isolated in leaves and fruit for pharmaceutical use. In addition to its antioxidant uses, chlorogenic acid is also known to slow glucose release into the blood, making it a possible preventative measure for both cardiovascular disease and type 2 diabetes. Chlorogenic acid is also showing promise in cancer treatment, inhibiting chemicals that contribute to tumor growth.[12] According to Dr. Cornelis, "Coffee is a primary source of chlorogenic acid for populations that consume a lot of coffee. That might have a beneficial impact on glucose levels which is a key kind of risk factor for type 2 diabetes.

Sanjiv Chopra, MD, is a professor of medicine at Beth Israel Deaconess Medical Center, and has published several books on healthy living, the latest being *The Big Five: Five Simple Things You Can Do to Live a Longer, Healthier Life*.[13] One of the five things is drinking coffee. Quite a bit of coffee, if you can manage it.

Is it caffeine that plays the major part in the health benefits of coffee? We really do not know. As Dr. Chopra explained in an interview, "Coffee has thousands of constituents, amongst them are kahweol and cafestol." Dr. Chopra said that experimental laboratory studies have shown that pretreatment with kahweol or cafestol abrogates injuries, especially to the liver.[14]

"Coffee also is very rich in chlorogenic acid, which is one of the richest antioxidants. Coffee is insulin sensitizing, so it helps in type 2 diabetes," explained Dr. Chopra. "If somebody already has type 2 diabetes and they drink two cups [of coffee] there's a 30 percent reduction in cardiovascular mortality. But we don't think it's the caffeine because I'm not aware of any good studies saying Coca-Cola, caffeine pills, tea, are healthy." There's a lot of hullabaloo about tea and green tea being rich in antioxidants, but Dr. Chopra said that he had yet to see a good study.

Coffee can be advantageous to health in other ways. "Coffee drinkers also have lower levels of something called TNF-alpha, tumor necrosis factor alpha; and CRP, C-reactive protein," Dr. Chopra said. "C-reactive protein is a risk factor for coronary artery disease. We don't really know the mechanism, but when there are dozens and dozens of studies, and when there's a dose-dependent effect, then it's a wake-up call, then we have to say, hmm, intriguing, believable." Dr. Chopra was impressed by a study published in the *New England Journal of Medicine* that found "coffee drinkers, men and women, have lower total and cause specific mortality."[15]

As for what coffee might have to do with heart attacks and stroke, and what component of the coffee is responsible for any effect, Dr. Cornelis said that while we really don't know, recent research suggests that coffee might be beneficial for preventing those outcomes. "In terms of my research," she explained, "I actually take a different approach. I think that the health effects of coffee or caffeine itself might actually vary by our ability to metabolize caffeine." The amount of coffee that one person needs to drink in order to ward off a certain disease might be very different from the amount another person might need to consume in order for the coffee to offer any kind of protection against the illness or condition.[16]

There is no firm conclusion as to whether chlorogenic acids affect the flavor of coffee in any way. As mentioned before, chlorogenic acid is a phenolic compound that has antioxidant and other benefits and seems to help with regulating blood sugar.

One factor that might affect how much the body benefits from drinking coffee is the roast of the coffee. But there are no firm conclusions about this and it is still under investigation. Some studies suggest that there might be more chlorogenic acid in light roasted coffee, so therefore light roast coffees might be more beneficial with respect to helping the body ward off some diseases and conditions.[17] On the other hand, there are more melanoids in darker roasts. Melanoids might help fight off some cancers, inflammation, and maybe even hypertension to some degree.[18]

Some studies have found that darker roasts are more effective than lighter roasts when it comes to bestowing added health benefits. The title of a study in *Molecular Nutrition and Food Research*, "Dark roast coffee is more effective than light roast coffee in reducing body weight, and in restoring red blood cell vitamin E and glutathione concentrations in healthy volunteers," speaks for itself.[19]

No one can really say for sure, however, which roast—light or dark—offers the most overall health benefits. There has to be more research, asserted Dr. Chopra. The studies out there are, he said, what are called epidemiological. A researcher asks questions, such as, "Do you drink coffee, yes or no? Do you drink regular or decaf? How many cups of coffee do you drink in a day?" Dr. Chopra continued, "Whether putting [in] cream or milk or sugar, whether it's organic coffee or pure coffee with more pure constituents, no one's done that study and I don't think it'll ever get done."

But what about the melanoids in darker roasts? Dr. Chopra said they don't translate into health benefits unless you conduct a study: "You can have something that says this is helpful and then the way we study it in medicine is you do a placebo control, randomized trial, [and] blind, where the investigator doesn't know which subjects are getting the active and which are getting the placebo, and the patients don't know. Then a study monitor assesses it and at the end you look at the results." But, he said, this will never happen with coffee. Can you have ten thousand subjects and tell five thousand of them that they can't drink coffee and the other five thousand that they should drink coffee, and then out of those, half of them must drink this kind of coffee and the other half must drink that kind of coffee, and drink the coffee a certain way and at a certain time? It is just not feasible.[20]

But we are discovering more about coffee's health benefits, and how caffeine affects coffee drinkers. Dr. Cornelis has always been interested in the genetics and, she said, we know that there is a genetic component to coffee consumption. "The genetic components are really pointing to our ability to metabolize caffeine. In general," she added, "what I mean by caffeine metabolism is that if individuals who are genetically predisposed to, who genetically kind of have this genetic signature in that they metabolize caffeine quickly, those same individuals are consuming more coffee or caffeine in general."

Dr. Cornelis's literature shows that these genetics that alter our metabolism ultimately impact our behavior, so people are naturally titrating their levels accordingly. There is no easy way to test to see if you are getting the right amount of caffeine for your metabolism. Dr. Cornelis said, "We tend to consume as much as we need. I think you can probably relate that if you are a coffee consumer you know when you might need a coffee because you're either feeling tired or sleepy. You have a cup of coffee and then you know generally how much you need to consume. That's kind of a learned experience . . . it's just interesting that there is a genetic component to that but we generally just go by feel."

Harvard researchers are also looking into what else is behind the benefits of coffee. It seems that decaffeinated coffee might have some of the same benefits as caffeinated coffee so the magic elements have to be something besides caffeine.

Dr. Cornelis added that these studies suggest that it's the non-caffeine components of coffee that affects type 2 diabetes..."partly because you kind of see the same protective effect of coffee on type 2 diabetes with decaf coffee and also with other studies that looked at the impact of caffeine on glucose levels, interestingly and paradoxically the caffeine has adverse effects on glucose."

Dr. Chopra's book *The Big 5* discusses many of the health benefits of coffee. Elizabeth Blackburn, PhD, who, with two colleagues, was awarded the Nobel Prize in medicine of physiology for discovering telomeres and telomerase.[21] As Dr. Chopra wrote in his book, "Just like we have a plastic tip on the end of shoelaces, there is a cap on the end of chromosomes called a telomere. Shortened telomeres and decreased telomerase activity is associated with cell aging."[22] Dr. Chopra added, "Now there's a study, I think in the last six months, [that shows] coffee drinkers have longer telomeres."[23]

Is it possible to drink decaffeinated coffee and still get the health benefits? "Decaffeinated coffee seems to have similar health benefits, except for cirrhosis of the liver," Dr. Chopra said. "There, for some reason, protection is seen with regular coffee and not decaf coffee." He specializes in hepatology, the field of liver disease.

Dr. Chopra explained, using the example of alcoholic cirrhosis, "Now for decades, we've been mystified, how come some people drink a pint of whiskey a day for twenty years and at the end of twenty years, 20 percent get cirrhosis? Is it their genes? Is it the way they metabolize alcohol through an enzyme called alcoholic dehydrogenase? The answer is coffee. If you drink that much [alcohol] and drink one cup of coffee a day, [there's a] 20 percent reduction in the chance of getting alcoholic cirrhosis, two cups, 40 percent, four cups, 80 percent."

"We have a very busy liver service at the Beth Israel Deaconess Medical Center, with very sick patients, pre- and post-transplants, and have taught all the residents and fellows, students, to ask every patient about coffee," Dr. Chopra said. "Week after week, during the last many years, I've sat down for rounds and they tell me about the five admissions and so on, and they say, 'Dr. Chopra, nobody drinks coffee.' One day I sat down, and the intern had a grin on his face, and he said, 'We finally have a patient who drinks coffee. And we asked him whether it's regular or decaf because you taught us it has to be regular, and it's regular coffee.'"

Then the intern asked the patient who said he drank coffee how many cups he drank a day and he answered four cups, four good-sized cups. "So," Dr. Chopra said, "you know, these epidemiological studies, they make excellent explanations, but I'll take my own history. And we go for rounds, they introduce me, I sit down, I take a detailed history, at the end I said, tell me about tea and coffee. He said, 'Doc, I don't drink tea, I love coffee.' I said, what do you drink? He said, 'Well, I go to drink coffee, I got to drink the real stuff.' I said, how many cups? He says, 'Four cups.' I said, what size, and he pointed to a paper cup, about eight ounces. And I asked one more question, how long have you been drinking coffee? He said, 'Since my liver transplant.' And the house staff fell down. That's the art of history taking."

Dr. Chopra continued, "He said, 'I never liked coffee. I got my liver transplant. I don't know what happened, I have a craving for coffee. Should I stop it?' I said, no, no, keep drinking it. So he was in, not for recurrent liver disease, he was in for bad cellulitis and because they're immunosuppressed we take it seriously and admit them and treat them. I have yet to come across a patient who drank four, five cups of coffee a day, regular coffee a day, and wound up with bad liver disease, if he or she had been doing it for many years. I'm a liver specialist so I got intrigued about this twenty-five years ago."

Migraines

When it comes to pain in the head, caffeine is both a culprit and a cure, according to WebMD and Cleveland Clinic.[24, 25] Quite a few pain relievers have caffeine as an ingredient (i.e., Excedrin Migraine, Anacin). Caffeine can improve the success of an analgesic by 40 percent. And there are also occasions when a headache might be vanquished with just caffeine alone.

Parkinson's Disease

According to a study headed by Alberto Ascherio, professor of Epidemiology and Nutrition at Harvard T. H. Chan School of Public Health, having four to five cups of java a day can nearly halve the possibility of getting Parkinson's Disease, as opposed to those who drink little or no caffeine.[26]

Cardiovascular Disease

In his book *The Big Five*, Dr. Chopra refers to a Harvard study done with researchers from Universidad Autónoma de Madrid that examined the possible link between coffee and strokes in women. Researchers found that: "women who drank two or more cups day reduced the risk of stroke by 19 percent—and the more coffee they drank the greater the reduction in risk."[27]

Nonsmoking women who drank four-plus cups of coffee were even better off, and had a 43 percent reduction in stroke incidence. And it doesn't seem to be the caffeine in the coffee that is the reason, since those who drank tea or other beverages with caffeine did not see the benefits, while those who drank two-plus cups of decaffeinated coffee did.[28, 29]

Depression

A 2011 Harvard School of Public Health's Department of Nutrition study showed that women who drank caffeinated coffee had a 20 percent lower risk of getting depression than women who did not drink coffee.[30, 31, 32]

Dementia

Researchers at Indiana University at Bloomington led by Hui-Chen Lu identified twenty-four compounds that might potentially boost the brain enzyme, NMNAT2, which has been shown to defend against dementia.

One of the compounds is caffeine and that is what the team focused on for the study. According to Hui-Chen Lu, more research on the other twenty-three compounds needs to be done and how they affect the brain.[33]

Single Serve for Portion Control?

Here is where the single-serve option found a niche—those who want to drink more coffee but don't want to drink it all at once, so a single-serve option fulfills a need here. Folks could drink more coffee and every time they had a cup, it would be fresh. And the coffee lover can try different brands, blends, and roasts with each cup of coffee. No committing to a whole pot.

Coffee drinking in studies usually refers to black coffee. You can't add fatty creamers and load on the sugar and expect to end up with anything remotely resembling a healthy cup of coffee. Something to keep in mind.

About health benefits, if you are trying to decide between getting the health benefits from a glass of wine or a cup of coffee, now you can have both at the same time, in one cup. With all the press about the benefits of resveratrol, a beneficial antioxidant found in red wine that is said to protect the heart and blood flow, it is not surprising that some coffee companies decided to combine resveratrol with coffee. Vera Roasting Company, founded by organic chemist Glen Miller, offers whole bean, ground, and single-serve coffee—CoffVee—consisting of 100 percent arabica beans infused with resveratrol after roasting. Molinari Private Reserve offers wine-infused coffee, a "full-bodied coffee [that] relaxes in a beautiful wine, absorbing the wine's nose and history . . ." in half-pound bags.

Drink Less—It Might Not Be So Good for You!

Caffeine usually reaches peak level in the blood an hour after drinking a cup of coffee, according to the FDA.[34] The caffeine then percolates around in your blood for about four to six hours. Drinking coffee every day causes a tolerance and you may need to drink more to feel the same energizing effects of the caffeine. And, because people metabolize caffeine at different rates, what might be not enough caffeine for one person may be too much for another. And if it is something other than the caffeine in coffee that provides health benefits, maybe decaf would provide the health benefits coffee drinkers are hoping for as an added bonus?

With digestion, coffee can increase acid and can cause heartburn—Dr. Chopra wrote about these not-so-good side effects of coffee in *The Big 5*. He said that coffee can cause gastroesophageal reflux disease, heartburn, and that is the same whether it's regular or decaf. And irritable bowel syndrome. Insomnia, tachycardia, tremor[s], it goes on."[35]

Coffee can affect sleep patterns, obviously, so that can be a negative in some situations. Drinking too much caffeinated coffee—say around five cups a day—can lead to caffeine withdrawal when the coffee lover suddenly puts the brakes on their daily habit.[36] Caffeine is also a diuretic, and too much can cause dehydration and dry, wrinkly skin. So, just drink more water, right? Finally, crashing from too much caffeine can lead to cravings for sweets, as can the idea that having a cup of coffee means having a little something to go along with it, like a doughnut or a piece of cake.

One gourmet method for making coffee has been found to be not so healthy: the French press. Diterpenes (or diterpenoids) are a class of chemical compounds that are found in coffee that help give the bean an oily richness. They are not so good for you. They are normally trapped in a coffee filter, which the French press does not use. Diterpenes could raise LDL (bad) cholesterol levels.

Dr. Cornelis agreed: "Actually that was actually shown several years ago. They found that boiled coffee, which isn't traditionally consumed now, boiled coffee contained particular lipids. They're actually called diterpenoids. Those lipids that were not removed from the coffee, those gave rise to increased cholesterol levels. That's pretty consistent and has been shown in trials. With filtering the coffee, those particular lipids are unfiltered in the coffee so that wouldn't have any impact on cholesterol."

Single Serve Might Make Sense
When You Want to Drink Less

Need to drink less coffee? The single serve can offer a convenient and quick way to imbibe a specific amount at measured intervals throughout the day and evening and the coffee drinker can still have a cup that is freshly brewed, regular or decaf. Said Dr. Cornelis: ". . . we know from the single serve versus, say, what you get from Starbucks or from a coffee pot more generally is that it's pretty controlled. You kind of control the amount of coffee that you're having and possibly the components of coffee. For example, we know that the amount of caffeine in coffee can vary by coffee cups."

Dr. Cornelis points to literature showing that even at the same coffeehouse, if one person gets a cup of coffee and then returns an hour or two later and gets the same size, if the caffeine content of those two coffees is measured, despite being the same size they might have different caffeine levels. "Clearly there [are] some differences in making the brewed coffee," she said. "It could vary, but with those single packets that's a particular amount of coffee and you're brewing it and you're drinking it right away. There's more of a control with the single serve."

CHAPTER 12

Does Single Serve Fuel Too Much Separateness?

When Keurig decided to take its single-serve brewer to the home market, it was the beginning of a sea change in not only how people consumed coffee, but in how they *thought about* coffee. In the office, the single serve fulfilled a purpose—providing people in the workplace with fresh-brewed coffee no matter what the time of day. This would lead to more efficiency since workers would take fewer outside breaks to get a decent cup of coffee. It was right there in the office.

But in the home—what was the point? It likely was that the time families spent together was becoming increasingly fractured. People in a household would awaken at different times, and go off to work, school, or wherever at different times. Having everyone on hand simultaneously (or near enough to ensure that the coffee sitting in the coffeemaker on the kitchen counter was not getting over-brewed or depleted) was happening less frequently at breakfast, lunch, or dinner. Household members were becoming more scattered and unpredictable when it came to when they would be where.

Sure, the K-Cup/single serve in the office provided a way for workers to get a decent cup of coffee without venturing far from their cubicle. And coffee is an integral part of the workplace environment. With more members of households being at home at different times, it naturally followed that what worked in the office as far as having a fresh-brewed cup of coffee available would work in the home.

And coffee is very important in the workplace. According to a story in the *Harvard Business Review*, "Workspaces that Move People," the most productive office space is one that promotes interaction among the people who work there, and not just the workers in a specialized area or department.[1] Another *Harvard Business Review* article, "The New Science of Building Great Teams," shows that communication among workers from many departments in a company or organization is essential to "sociometrics," how people and teams communicate with one another throughout a company. Poor sociometrics often results in poor communication and fewer new ideas.[2] The Norwegian telecommunications company Telenor was looking for ways to increase engagement among the different components of its workforce. According to "Workspaces that Move People," "The data collected over some weeks showed that when a salesperson increased interactions with coworkers on other teams—that is, increased exploration—by 10%, his or her sales also grew by 10% . . ."[3]

But what would be a way to set things up so the folks from the advertising department, for example, could interact on a regular basis with workers from the art department?

> In this case, the answer lay with coffee. At the time, the company had roughly one coffee machine for every six employees, and the same people used the same machines every day. The sales force commiserated with itself. Marketing people talked to marketing people. The company invested several hundred thousand dollars to rip out the coffee stations and build fewer, bigger ones—just one for every 120 employees.[4]

Having the coffee brewers in strategically located places that would provide a reason for employees to go there—to get a cup of coffee—would serve as a place for workers from different areas of the company to happen to meet, resulting in a chance for people from other departments to hear about what was going on in other areas of the company. Some companies might provide a large, open space for people to gather but this is more forced and not conducive to a casual and frequent exchange among different workers like going to a coffee-brewing station is.[5]

So coffee can have a real effect on the workplace. The coffee machine can be a place where people from different departments brew a cup of coffee and, at the same time, have a chat with someone from another department that they otherwise might never had run into. This provides a healthy and productive "cross pollination" of ideas.

As for what kind of coffee brewing system most workers prefer, the 2017 National Coffee Drinking Trends Study published by the National Coffee Association found that while espresso machines were the most desired option for in-office coffee preparation, single-cup brewers came in second, with instant coffee coming in third and the drip coffeemaker coming in last.[6]

Since the single serve is the second-most popular, was productivity's gain socialization's loss? Maybe stepping out for ten or fifteen minutes with another colleague from their own or a different department was healthier in the long run. Conversing with colleagues while going out for a change of scenery and different air can be recharging and certainly more productive socially. Even stepping out of the office alone has long-term benefits.

Take Dr. Cornelis and her experience, for example. In her workplace, there is no coffeemaker in her personal office but there is a single-serve coffee brewer in the office kitchen. She remarked how she would go to the kitchen in the office and if people were there, she would interact with them while she used the coffeemaker.

She mentioned someone else who gets coffee another way, a colleague who doesn't have access to a single-serve brewer and goes outside the office for coffee at a nearby Starbucks. This is obviously a very different experience than just going down the hall to make a single cup of coffee. This colleague is probably getting more exercise and possibly running into people at the Starbucks at different times. Using the brewer at the office means getting just minimal exercise walking to the kitchen.

Despite the popularity of the single serve, at home and in the workplace, specialty coffee shops continue to thrive and do a brisk brew business. As Heather Ward, Market Research Manager with the Specialty Coffee Association of America wrote, "SCAA's latest consumer research study, conducted in early 2016, presented data that showed that although the majority of consumers still drink coffee at home, 94 percent of the study's respondents also drink coffee at a coffee shop."[7] And while the sharp growth of coffee shops is slowing a bit, the number of shops has risen by almost 50 percent and more people are drinking gourmet coffee.

"Specialty coffee shops," added Ward, "play a key role in shaping the consumer experience . . . In past SCAA research, specialty coffee consumers have consistently revealed the significance of their coffee shop experiences. They associate their coffee with social interactions, and they love the sense of belonging that comes from the barista knowing their name or remembering their favorite drink. Their relationship with coffee is deeply personal, and the human interaction that takes place in a coffee shop enhances the emotional connection and overall experience." [8]

It's a Brew Ha Ha

One of the many examples of how a coffee shop can be a social connector is found in the Northwest corner of Pennsylvania. In 2015, Cathie Riehl McMillin started Brew Ha Ha at the Colony in Erie, Pennsylvania, recently named number three in the list of "The Ten Coolest Coffee Shops in Pennsylvania."[9] She wanted the experience to be like having coffee at home—with family and friends—with the best coffee you could get in Erie and with some accompaniments that you would not find in a big brand-name coffee shop.

Riehl McMillin says she knows at least 50 percent of the customers by name, and the place is bicycle and dog friendly. "Dogs are welcome on the outdoor deck and sidewalk table areas," she said. "They get water and biscuits. Many people bring rescue dogs and puppies for socialization, as well as for themselves. We have 'honor' coffee where you can throw down two bucks in a jar and help yourself to a medium coffee to go, with no waiting in line."[10]

They roast the coffee onsite and the staff take time with customers who ask questions, and educate them about the origins of the beans, how they roast, etc. "People love that," Riehl McMillin said. "So, I guess I opened a coffee shop for myself and the patrons. A place that I would like to visit, with the philosophy of serving the freshest, most varied, and delicious coffee and food. Being smaller, we are able to customize people's drinks and work with them to satisfy their coffee needs."

Shops to get a good cup of coffee and socialize will always be around. It is a place to not only get coffee, but to see what is going on, much like those then controversial coffee shops that sprang up centuries ago.

Does Single Serve Brew Loneliness?

What does it say, if anything, about the individual versus the group—even family—brewing and drinking coffee using the single serve as a one-at-a time, just-for-me method?

It depends upon whom you ask. About how single-serve coffee brewers with their one-cup-at-a-time focus can exacerbate isolation, Dr. Rebecca Nowland, psychologist and Senior Lecturer at the University of Bolton, UK, said she is not sure how much this situation actually contributes to isolation or loneliness. She sees this as more of a cultural shift to be more and more individualistic and independent.

"I wouldn't put too much emphasis on this for making loneliness or isolation worse particularly but it may be a result of a move towards a more individualistic culture," Dr. Nowland said. "It also may be the result of employers not really wanting people to socialize at work and increase the productivity of staff."[11]

While you can have a virtual coffee klatch with social media friends and contacts, the one-on-one interaction of sharing a cup of java and ideas or experiences is not there. And at the office, there is no more gathering around the office coffee pot for whatever reason, to complain about who didn't make a fresh pot of coffee, or left the mostly unfilled glass pot on the warm burner so that what was in the pot looked like, and probably tasted like, melted tar. The terrible coffee that no one would be held accountable for. Maybe single serve in the office is a viable option. But so is stepping outside to a specialty coffee shop for a few minutes.

And at home, there seems to be little time anyway for family to gather as a group so the single serve probably makes sense. Family members come and go separately, taking their mugs of coffee with them and heading off.

Of course, you can have speed and an individually-prepared coffee shop coffee at the same time with minimal human contact. Starbucks, Dunkin' Donuts, Intelligentsia, and others have apps that allow the coffee lover to order on the go and not have to wait while the drink is being prepared. Place the order and, by the time you get to the coffee shop, the order is waiting for you.

Full Circle

Ironically, in 2015 Keurig came out with an option that is almost a throwback to making coffee by the potful, the K-Carafe, which makes a carafe of coffee, for home use. (Back in 2013, they offered the Keurig Bolt, since discontinued, which made a pot of coffee, mainly for offices.) So, in some way, we have come full circle. Now you can use the method that was invented to make one cup of coffee at a time to make a pot of coffee that makes up to five servings at a time. The K-Carafe pod is also recyclable.

So now you can make a pot of coffee from a giant K-Carafe pod.

A pot of coffee. It is almost like a throwback to the past. Almost.

CHAPTER 13

Just What is Single Serve Anyway?

While single-serve coffee usually means those one-time-use coffee pods or cups, not everyone thinks this or agrees that this is a way to make a good cup of coffee.

Mané Alves, a native of Lisbon, Portugal, has worked in the wine and coffee industries for over twenty-five years. He travels extensively to coffee-producing countries throughout Central America, South America, Africa, and conducts calibration tests, teaches seminars on coffee production and quality standards, and offers Q Grader courses (A Q Grader is someone who has received credentials from the Coffee Quality Institute to grade and score coffees using the standards that the Specialty Coffee Association of America has developed).[1] You know that he is not going to suffer single-serve coffee pods gladly. But, he understands.

Manés Alves views single-serve coffee this way: "There [are] two ways to serve the single serve. One, is if you are just looking at what is out there in the marketplace, most of the single serve that's in the marketplace are things that are like Keurig cups. There's other systems besides Keurig. That is a step up in terms of availability, but it's not a step up in terms of quality. It's easy." But, as he pointed out, there are other problems. One obviously being the issues with landfill and waste. While the majority of these cups are not recyclable, Alves feels that the cups that are recyclable require so much work to recycle them, that most customers just don't do it.[2]

"The reason they buy those cups is because it's easy," he reasoned. "Not because they have to do twenty steps to recycle. Otherwise they would just do coffee normally." While he sees that convenience as an asset of the single serve, he doesn't consider single serve comparable to specialty coffee. "In terms of the specialty side, I don't consider that specialty. That is mass market."

On the specialty side, there are a lot of cafés that will brew a cup of a specialty coffee that is ground and brewed upon the customer's order. The customer can ask for almost anything.

"I'll give you an example." explained Alves. "If you go to a supermarket and you see a coffee that sells for twenty-five dollars, you'll probably cringe and run away. If you go to a café and someone gives you a coffee for four bucks, well, the vast majority of people are already paying four bucks at Starbucks for a cup of coffee or cappuccino or whatever. If someone gives you a straight cup of coffee, that of course, if you want to add milk you can, but it would be a crime, but a coffee that is an incredible coffee in terms of taste, and that we can sell that for four bucks, then it's completely different than a market that was not accessible to the customers before." These options did not exist a couple years ago, at least on a wide scale.

Alves believes that it all depends on expectations and how much effort a coffee drinker wants to put into getting that first cup of coffee in the morning. "If you need to have the coffee ready by the time you put your foot out of bed, then you want to buy an automatic machine that grinds and prepares the coffee [using a timer]," he said. "Usually that doesn't produce a lot of good coffee. If you can do two steps, then you have a much better cup of coffee. If you can do three steps, meaning, if you have the coffee, you grind the coffee, you put it through the brewer, then you get an even better cup of coffee." So if you put more effort into preparing the coffee, you will get a better cup of coffee.

But Alves is realistic. "We know the vast majority of people want to have everything ready," he said. "They don't want to deal with it. They want a good cup of coffee, but they don't want to deal with anything. If they're conscious in terms of throwing the steps away, if they don't care at that level either, so that would be easy for them to go with a K-Cup style."

Intelligentsia Coffee, founded in 1995 by Doug Zell and Emily Mange, has roasting works, training labs, and coffee bars in about five cities in the United States. Now Intelligentsia is a part of JAB Holding. Andrew Atkinson, Intelligentsia's Retail Regional Manager of New Markets & East Coast, as well as their Green Coffee Buyer, said that Intelligentsia won't consider the single serve like a K-Cup any time in the foreseeable future. "I think it would really have to come a long way I think technology-wise for us to feel comfortable putting something out there like that." He said that right now K-Cups are difficult. It is difficult to brew excellent coffee using them, since it is an automated process. The machine has control, and the company creating the pods and the machine that's making the coffee has control over the inherent quality. "You suddenly remove the personal dial-in of the coffee or the creation of the recipe of the coffee from the person and you're suddenly sticking your name on something that should inherently have automatic qualities or the quality will be purely dictated by a machine and a pot," Atkinson said. "The technology doesn't exist yet for us to be able to do that and hit the sufficient quality marks we would want to." Atkinson thinks that single serve can be thought of in a nonautomated way, for example, brewing a single cup using a Chemex, a coffee preparation device that uses the infusion method (similar to the drip method).[3]

Intelligentsia opened a coffee bar and retail store in Chicago and roasted their own coffee in the store. Even though they had to use equipment that was on the antique side, they honed the coffee process until it was perfect. Atkinson said that their original roaster, Geoff Watts, developed their coffee-purchasing system. Geoff, he said, "really wanted to create a system in which there was more direct relationship and communication with producers, seeing that traditionally the use of importers created an inherent lack of accountability in communication both ways."

Watts started traveling to farms and, with Peter Giuliano (formerly of Counter Culture), developed Intelligentsia's coffee-buying program, his codification of what a direct trade relationship should be. Said Atkinson, "Direct trade really is our own internal branding of a coffee that meets certain criteria around transparent relationships and quality so it's not necessarily like a third-party certification that one can pick up."

Atkinson said that while everybody seems to use the term "direct trade," Geoff said he was going to have rules for the company that he was going to make public so people would know what it meant when they saw his direct trade sticker and logo on the bag. Counter Culture, said Atkinson, "developed that side-by-side, pretty well, and they have their own set of standards. But really, aside from those two, it's very difficult to say, well what does this whole direct trade thing mean, right?" Exactly. Direct trade can mean different things, depending on whom you ask.[4] The short answer is that with direct trade the producer interacts directly with the customer and they come to an understanding that benefits them both.[5]

Intelligentsia follows the coffee process every step of the way, from the very start to the coffee shop. Atkinson's main focus at Intelligentsia is retail in new markets but he is also a green coffee buyer for the company, so he does green coffee buying in El Salvador and so on. Intelligentsia's green coffee buying is set up so that no one person is a full-time coffee buyer but rather they pull people from different parts of the company to focus on one country, build relationships within that country, and then bring that coffee along its journey into their respective department.[6]

It is a lot about building and maintaining relationships, and Intelligentsia then selects the best lots of coffee from these relationships. "For example," Atkinson said, "when I start working with a coffee farmer, I'm down in El Salvador during the harvest process and you know we're there watching the harvest, working with the farmers, kind of understanding. All right, well, what were your difficulties this year? What are you hoping for this year? What are your goals and ideas? Okay, here are my goals and ideas. Let's collaborate together. Let's work together so that we can together create this really awesome product and kind of hold each other accountable and support each other in creating successful goals."

Intelligentsia at one time acted as its own importer. "We still coordinate all of our own international logistics," Atkinson said, "though at this time we do contract some logistics companies third party to handle the heavy lifting, but we are in constant communication with everybody who has our coffee at every single point and helping guide it along the process until it shows up here. So we really are there when the coffee's in its fruit and we guide it all the way to our retail stores."

Atkinson thinks that one of the things in the coffee business that has changed quite a bit is that there are a lot more resources, especially, he said, when you start looking at the past decade or so and the small businesses that have started. It has become very, very popular to be an entrepreneur, creating your own business, and using technology to do so. "Coffee as far as the purchasing side, has really kept up with that," he added. "You know, there [are] all sorts of resources that are available to make buying great coffee easier."

Atkinson thinks that there is also a risk with all of the technology and information people have at their disposal. For instance, he said, "I can go onto Coffee Shrub (a micro-seller of coffee that serves shops that roast) or Sweet Maria's (Sweet Maria's Home Coffee-Roasting) and I can say, 'Oh. I want that lot, that lot, that lot.' I know exactly where they're coming from. I can go down to the farm and take some pictures almost like kind of eco-tourism and I can call it direct trade."

Before, much of the risk with coffee was on the buyers choosing the best coffees. Now, according to Atkinson, a lot of the risk is on the farmers because they are dealing with smaller companies, and sometimes the farmers have no real guarantee that anyone's going to buy anything.

"There has been a shift in large-scale operations where farmers kind of know that they have an outlet for their coffee to the small-scale operations where it's a little bit more up in the air," Atkinson said. Adding to that is the constant reduction of crop yields and "the fact that every year it gets a little bit harder to actually grow coffee, especially quality coffee . . . and we need to start sharing some of this responsibility."

Do you like your coffee cold but you're not too thrilled by the usual selections of ready-made coffees in bottles and cans? Not overly fond of the mountains of ice that are dumped into a cup to make your request for an iced whatever? A solution exists, my friend. La Colombe Coffee Roasters is offering Draft Latte, a brainchild of CEO and Travel Channel coffee explorer Todd Carmichael, a canned latte with a twist born out of the cold lattes on tap that his stores are known for.[7] The secret is in the valve and the gas. A tiny hole covered by a plastic seal is on the bottom of the can. Using a patent-pending process, when the can is opened a rush of foam rises to the top. The result is a cold, café-style latte.

Cold coffee in a can is part of reason for coffee's global growth.[8] According to Jonny Forsyth, Global Drinks analyst at Mintel, a market intelligence firm:

> The global coffee industry continues to experience healthy growth, driven by Asian markets in particular. Asia has far more growth potential as traditionally tea drinking consumers are converted slowly but surely into coffee drinkers . . . In terms of local tastes, currently Asia Pacific leads the way in launches of ready-to-drink cold coffee. In 2016, 29% of all coffee launches in Asia Pacific were ready-to-drink cold coffee products, compared to just 10% in Europe . . .[9]

But you want your coffee quick and you want it hot. If you want another way make a cup of hot coffee, there is always the throwback to instant coffee. Instant coffee, however, with a bit more panache. Starbucks VIA offers single serve using a different method. Ready-brewed instant coffee? Is it instant or brewed? Or both? Does it have more in common with single-serve brew cups or with Maxwell House coffee singles? Starbucks VIA, introduced in 2009, seemed to eliminate any lingering "stigma" of instant coffee. In fact, instant coffee has become quite popular throughout the world.[10]

According to Euromonitor International, the world's leading independent provider of strategic market research, instant coffee is very popular in
some areas. Global Trends in Instant Coffee, a report by Matthew Barry
and Virginia Lee, reports that instant coffee, as of 2015, is a $28 billion
industry and has risen 7 percent from 2010 to 2015, and is the second
largest category of hot drinks (after fresh coffee, of course).[11] As for who
is drinking instant coffee, their research shows that Asia seems to be leading the way, with Iran second. This follows a natural pattern. According
to the report, specialty coffee shops created a coffee culture in traditional
tea-imbibing markets. The report stated instant coffee can grow at the
same time as single-serve coffee pods grow in these areas. As more instant
coffee becomes more inspired by specialty coffees, this type of coffee will
continue to be a popular option. In the United Kingdom, instant coffee is
the most popular way to consume coffee, the report concluded, but instant
will be surpassed by fresh brewed in that area by 2020. China remains an
untapped market full of possibilities.

According to Jonny Forsyth, Global Drinks Analyst at Mintel,

"Instant coffee still dominates the retail market in Asia. Two in five
(42%) coffee launches in Asia Pacific were soluble coffee granule products,
compared to just one in five (20%) launches in Europe and a mere 6% of
launches in North America in 2016."[12] Coffee pods, though, are not sitting
out the race. Forsyth said:

Globally, it is coffee pods which are causing the biggest stir. Pods
accounted for over one quarter (26%) of all global coffee retail innovation in 2016, up from 11% of launches in 2011. Although still
in its early stages in Asia Pacific, pod innovation is still showing
strong signs of growth in this region. Around one in eight (13%)
coffee products launched in 2016 was a coffee pod, up from 4% of
launches in this region in 2011.[13]

CHAPTER 14

What's Next for Coffee for One?

Ensuring Quality Control

Nothing stays the same and this is certainly true of how coffee drinkers brew their coffee and the form that coffee can take. Ensuring that the quality of single-serve coffee continues to improve is something that Coffee Enterprises' Spencer Turer knows about firsthand. "I think over the years we've probably tested dozens of brands in the single-serve category," he said. He referred to a project that Coffee Enterprises did for the National Coffee Association. They tested a 100 percent Colombian product in every single-cup brewer that was on the market at that time, doing a compare and contrast. Every month, Turer commented, there are new products coming online. There are numerous roasters getting into Nespresso-type pods and Coffee Enterprises has been doing a lot of testing for products in that platform. "I would be surprised if there's any respected brand or respected coffee brewing platform that we have not tested in the past," he said.

As for different uses that could be in the future for single serve, Turer said they are under confidentially agreements, but he can say that advancements are being made in brewing technology on the single-cup platform. "There [are] new developments in different types of brewers," he added, "and there's also a lot of interest in the single cup for high quality tea as well as cold brew products and trying to figure out how to capture the iced coffee, cold brew coffee trends, into consumer appliances and single cup machines."

An Unexpected Side of Single-Portion Coffee

Just because something is a bit unusual or unfamiliar doesn't mean that someday it won't be a part of everyday life. Remember all the gadgets that seemed preposterous in any number of movies about the future? For example, enough of the then-futuristic devices seen in *Back to the Future* are now in use that we should keep an open mind about ideas or breakthrough products that might seem too wacky at the moment.[1] Sometimes the outlandish prototype evolves into something more manageable, like how designers view what they show in fashion shows as being more directional than what will actually be worn.[2] Sometimes, a translation is involved. There are, of course, always exceptions. Here is a look at some coffee-centric products in various stages. How about chewable coffee? Not those dry, chalky coffee tablets. The Mintel 2017 Trends Report said: "For those who are extremely short of time in the morning, Go Cubes are gummy coffee bites made with real cold-brew coffee."[3] As the chewable coffee option's website says, "GO CUBES are the future of coffee. GO CUBES combine the kick of coffee with the relaxation of green tea. And instead of putting your coffee in a cup, you can put it in your pocket, for performance on the go."

Each single GO CUBE has a half a cup of coffee (50 mg caffeine) and nootropics, so you know how much caffeine you are getting. Each pack comes with an assortment of three flavors: Mocha, Pure Drip, and Latte.[4, 5]

How many GO CUBES should you eat at a time? The site recommends going by how many cups of coffee you usually drink at a time, and over time. The caffeine charge from a serving should last between four and five hours.

For another take on coffee as a beverage, there is Cafe from Soylent™ (Yes, like the portmanteau word—from soy and lentil—that appears in Harry Harrison's *Make Room! Make Room!* But *Soylent Green,* the film adapted from that novel, has a more sinister definition of the concoction).

This Soylent is a food technology pioneer that produces "convenient, complete foods designed to provide maximum nutrition with minimal effort."[6] In the case of Soylent Cafe, you can have your breakfast and drink your coffee, too, all at once—in one bottle. Their Cafe Coffiest and Cafe Vanilla, for example, contain real, lightly roasted coffee, according to their website.

A new venture by the name of Goat Story has designed a smart coffee brewer that combines traditional coffee brewing methods with the newest technology. The *Gina* has a built-in smart scale that ends the impreciseness of getting just the right amount of ingredients. This coffeemaker is connected to a mobile app. It tracks your brewing data and pilots you through the brewing routine. When you have finished, you can save your brew recipe and share it with your friends and family and other coffee lovers.

With *Gina*, you can choose from three different brewing methods—pour over, immersion, or cold drip. All you have to do is point the control to the correct amount of water flow. They also have an unusual-looking vessel, shaped like a goat horn, for carrying around and drinking your coffee. The company's website says this is in honor of the goat that discovered coffee.[7]

Here is a bit of an unexpected coffee-centric product from the United Kingdom, courtesy of the 2017 Trends Report, the Barisieur. Try to envision this. It is an alarm clock, yes. But it is an alarm clock designed to wake up the sleeping individual with the soothing sound of boiling water and the invigorating aroma of coffee (or tea, if you swing that way). The product is still in the design stage but it seems like it could definitely be an option for those who want to open their eyes and other senses along with the much-needed preparation of coffee. Everything would, of course, have to be prepared the night before, but that is not so difficult. There is a place for the beaker of water and siphon, the coffee cup, and the coffee-filled filter, all atop a timepiece that looks something like a clock radio from the 1970s.[8, 9] Sounds like a very pleasant way to wake up. As long as you don't absentmindedly try to hit a snooze button. Ouch!

As if automated coffee brewers weren't enough, there have recently been several stories about Robot Baristas. There they were in January 2017 at the Consumer Electronics Show, a Bosch cappuccino robot and a Denso coffee robot rivaling at a battle of the barista robots to see which could make the best coffee drinks. They did rather well. These do not seem to be electronics show gimmicks. San Francisco has a Robotic Café, Café X, which was started after the now CEO realized that much of the work that baristas do could be done by a robot.[10] It all seems to be working.[11]

Reconciling Single Serve with Brewing by the Pot

But back to the human way of brewing coffee. There seems to be a place for many brewing methods. After all, who has the luxury of a completely controlled or set-in-stone day or night? Sometimes we need and/or want one option for brewing coffee, and other times we need or want another method. Sometimes you feel like a single serve, sometimes you feel like a pot. Sometimes you want a quick fix and other times you want to be immersed in a more complex preparation.

For coffee drinkers who want a brewer that gives them more of a choice about not only what constitutes single serve, but also adjusts to the way they want to make coffee on any given day and in how large a quantity at a time, there are different types of brewers, from lower tech to ultra tech. Some brewers are giving coffee lovers the option of what method to use to brew a cup of coffee. Or a pot of coffee. From the same machine.

Spinn and BUNN coffeemakers offer a choice of brewing methods, serving coffee pods or ground coffee. These are two very different types of brewers, even just considering price point.[12]

BUNN's Single Cup My Café brewer takes single pods of various forms, yet it also allows the coffee lover to use ground coffee.[13] The brewer comes with separate drawers that work with either ground coffee, pod, or plain hot water for any other type of beverage, such as tea.

Spinn, which invites you to "Elevate Your Coffee," is a bit more complicated. And, according to their website, a lot more rewarding. The brewer grinds the beans, makes a pot of coffee, a single cup, or an espresso, and uses Wi-Fi so the coffee drinker can control everything with their phone.

According to their site, Spinn has connected features and a worldwide network of coffee roasters. The proprietary app allows users to precisely control every aspect of the brewing process or they can allow Spinn to handle the details with preprogrammed recipes and brewing methods recommended by professional roasters and baristas around the world.

When it comes to coffee, some folks like to make a pot of coffee because there is the potential for more people to enjoy it and it is available if someone else stops by. That same person will have a single-serve brewer and can honestly tell guests when one asks for regular coffee, and another has to have decaf, and still another can drink only tea, that it is no problem—they can have any of these selections and it is no bother.

As long as the people behind the single-serve method keep working toward a balance with the environmental issues, and everyone makes the conscious decision to choose fair trade, direct trade, and any other means of providing fairness to the coffee producers as well as the environment, choosing how we brew our coffee can safely and simply be a matter of personal preference.

The National Coffee Association's 2017 Coffee Drinking Trends report indicates that the coffee market is responding to the needs of a new generation and the impact of advancements in technology and coffee brewing. Keep finding new ways to brew and enjoy coffee. Life happens, as the adage goes, but coffee helps.

Tom Squitieri is an award-winning foreign correspondent, educator, father, poet, and star gazer who has enjoyed, brewed, been fueled by, and delighted many with coffee on all seven continents.

"One of the favorite stories I wrote from the Bosnian war was when the coffee houses of Sarajevo started coming back to life," he said. "Then the people knew the war was over." As one person told him:

Coffee without fear is the best in the world.

Acknowledgments

This book was a long time brewing and there are a lot of people to thank, starting with Skyhorse Publishing and my editor Caroline Russomanno. Thank you to E. R. Fallon for being an inimitable first reader and offering insightful suggestions.

People who may have been in the background but whose help proved invaluable, who helped either gather statistics or put me in touch with people to interview: Kate Kaplan, executive director at Oakland Coffee Works; Marissa Bosler, communications executive at Euromonitor; Jim Zelinski at Zelinski PR; Tara Smith, director of marketing, and Heather Ward, market research manager at the Specialty Coffee Association; Joe DeRupo, External Relations & Communications director of the National Coffee Association; Katharine Olsen, account executive at Weber Shandwick; Kate Buerba at Laughing Man Coffee; Kevin Gaydosh at Obrien Et Al. Advertising; Karen Noonan, Global Corporate Affairs manager for Mars Drinks; Jennifer Traegar at Traeger Communications; Nicole Myers at Soylent; Brian Kubicki at Massimo Zanetti Beverage; and Stefan Kanfer for his helpful feedback.

And a very special thanks to my family for being there and to my adopted dog for being okay with a little less playtime while I was working on this book.

Endnotes

Preface

1. The National Coffee Association USA, Inc., "NCA 2016 Single Cup Brewing, Changing Behaviors and Attitudes," (New York: 2017).
2. The National Coffee Association USA, Inc., "National Coffee Drinking Trends 2017," (New York: 2017).

Introduction

1. B. Lillie, "Italian Coffee Culture," *Italy Magazine,* 4 Nov 2013, [Online], Available: http://www.italymagazine.com/featured-story/italian-coffee-culture. [Accessed March 2017].

Chapter 1—Coffee Consumption; from Flat to Flat White

1. "Beer for Breakfast," History is Served, March 2017, [Online], Available: http://recipes.history.org/2014/09/beer-for-breakfast/, [Accessed March 2017].
2. J. B. and S. Haley, "Coffee Consumption over the Last Century," 1 June 2007. [Online], Available: https://www.ers.usda.gov/amber-waves/2007/june/coffee-consumption-over-the-last-century/, [Accessed March 2017].
3. "A Morning Cola Instead of Coffee?," *The New York Times,* 20 Jan 1988, [Online], Available: http://www.nytimes.com/1988/01/20/business/a-morning-cola-instead-of-coffee.html, [Accessed Jan 2017].
4. "Alternative Caffeine Fix: Coke if Popping Up on the Morning Menu," *LA Times* from *The Washington Post,* 2 Dec 1987, [Online], Available: http://articles.latimes.com/1987-12-02/business/fi-17237_1_coke. [Accessed Jan 2017].
5. R. Obias, "Mental Floss," March 2017, [Online], Available: http://mentalfloss.com/article/66433/12-discontinued-products-coca-cola-and-pepsi. [Accessed March 2017].

6. Cafe Cola, http://cafecola.com/product.html.

7. T. Danovich, "Why Big Soda Is Still Fighting for a Place at the Breakfast Table," 15 Feb 2016, [Online], Available: http://www.eater.com/2016/2/15/10976654/breakfast-soda-drinking-trend. [Accessed Feb 2007].

8. "Bring Back Jolt," https://www.facebook.com/pg/bringbackjolt/about/?ref=page_internal, [Accessed Sept. 2017].

9. "History of the Coffeemaker," Feb 2017, [Online], Available: http://www.coffee.org/History-of-the-Coffee-Maker. [Accessed Feb 2017].

10. C. Marshall, *The Guardian*, 14 May 2015, [Online], Available: https://www.theguardian.com/cities/2015/may/14/the-first-starbucks-coffee-shop-seattle-a-history-of-cities-in-50-buildings-day-36 [Accessed Jan 2017].

11. W. Roseberry, "The Rise of Yuppie Coffees and the Reimagination of Class in the United States," *American Anthropologist*, vol. 98, pp. 762–774, 1996.

12. L. Rohter, *The Washington Post*, 24 June 1979, [Online], Available: https://www.washingtonpost.com/archive/politics/1979/06/24/brazil-awaits-full-impact-of-early-frost-in-coffee-areas/1476ca19-39ff-493f-b0e2-fabed0b9295f/?utm_term=.b645e6db95cb, [Accessed Jan 2017].

13. "Coffee Research," [Online], Available: http://www.coffeeresearch.org/market/frosthistory.htm, [Accessed Jan 2017].

14. UPI, "UPI," 28 July 1981, [Online], Available: http://www.upi.com/Archives/1981/07/28/Brazilian-frost-less-damaging-than-1975/4715365140800/. [Accessed Jan 2017].

15. "International Coffee Organization," 2017, [Online], Available: http://www.ico.org/icohistory_e.asp. [Accessed Jan 2017].

16. "U.S. Coffee Drinking Slips after Slight Gain; Young Still not Drinking," *World Coffee & Tea*, pp. 21–22, 1980.

17. "U.S. Coffee Drinking Slips."

18. "Ad Man Cautions Coffee Men to Modernize Coffee's Image; Sees Coffee as Drink of the '80s," *World Coffee & Tea*, pp. 76–78, 1981.

19. Rosenberry, "The Rise of Yuppie Coffees."

20. National Coffee Association USA, "Coffee Roast Guide," March 2017, [Online], Available: http://www.ncausa.org/About-Coffee/Coffee-Roasts-Guide, [Accessed March 2017].

21. Pacific Bag, Inc., "One-Way Degassing Valve, What Is it?," March 2017, [Online], Available: https://www.pacificbag.com/blog/2015/7/8/one-way-degassing-valve-what-is-it, [Accessed March 2017].

22. Pacific Bag, Inc., "One-Way Degassing Valve."

23. Pacific Bag, Inc, "A History of Coffee Bags," March 2017, [Online], Available: https://www.pacificbag.com/blog/2015/7/8/a-history-of-coffee-bags, [Accessed March 2017].

24. Specialty Coffee Association, "Because Great Coffee Doesn't Just Happen," March 2017, [Online], Available: http://scaa.org/?page=work, [Accessed March 2017].

25. Coffee & Cocoa International, "Giants Clash in Specialty Brands War. Coffee and Cocoa International," 13(5):9., *C&CI*, 1986.

26. N. Yoshihara, *The Los Angeles Times,* 3 Dec 1986, [Online], Available: http://articles.latimes.com/1986-12-03/business/fi-293_1_coffee-market. [Accessed March 2017].

27. Corporate site [Online] Available: http://www.eightoclock.com/story, [Accessed March 2017].

28. M. Alves, Interviewee, [Interview], Feb. 23, 2017.

29. University site [Online] Available: https://coffeecenter.ucdavis.edu/, [Accessed March 2017].

Chapter 2—A Sixty-Second Take on the Sometimes-Subversive Journey of Coffee through History

1. "History of Coffee," [Online], Available: http://www.ethiopianspecialtycoffee.com/history.htm, [Accessed Jan 2017].

2. Selamta, April through June 1996, [Online], Available: http://www.selamta.net/Ethiopian%20Coffee.htm. [Accessed February 2017].

3. Selamta, April through June 1996.

4. NCA, "The History of Coffee," 2017, [Online], Available: http://www.ncausa.org/About-Coffee/History-of-Coffee, [Accessed Feb. 2017].

5. NCA, "Histroy of Coffee."

6. Selamta, April through June 1996.

7. Selamta, April through June 1996.

8. Corporate site [Online] Available: https://www.caffeflorian.com/en/, [Accessed March 2017].

9. "LLoyds of London Corporate History," March 2017, [Online], Available: https://www.lloyds.com/lloyds/about-us/history/corporate-history. [Accessed Feb 2017].

10. NCA, "The History of Coffee."

11. NCA, "The History of Coffee."

12. NCA, "The History of Coffee."

13. "The History of Coffee in Brazil," March 2017, [Online], Available: http://www.casabrasilcoffees.com/learn/history-of-coffee-in-brazil/, [Accessed March 2017].

14. World Atlas, [Online], NCA, Available: http://www.worldatlas.com/articles /top-coffee-producing-countries.html, [Accessed Feb 2017].
15. NCA, "The History of Coffee."

Chapter 3—The Journey from Tree to Table

1. NCA, "10 Steps from Seed to Cup," March 2017, [Online], Available: http://www .ncausa.org/About-Coffee/10-Steps-from-Seed-to-Cup. [Accessed March 2017].
2. NCA, "What is Coffee?" http://www.ncausa.org/About-Coffee/What-is-Coffee, [Accessed Sept 2017].
3. NCA, "10 Steps."
4. NCA, "10 Steps."
5. NCA, "10 Steps."
6. NCA, "10 Steps."
7. "Cupping Protocols," March 2017, [Online], Available: http://www.scaa .org/?page=resources&d=cupping-protocols. [Accessed March 2017].
8. NCA, "10 Steps."
9. NCA, "10 Steps."
10. "Coffee Lab Intl.," Feb 2017, [Online], Available: http://www.coffeelab.com /quality-assurance—coffee-testing.html. [Accessed Feb 2017].
11. M. Alves, Interviewee, [Interview], Feb. 23, 2017.

Chapter 4—Rise of the Single Serve

1. N. Lazaris, Interviewee, [Interview], 17 Jan 2017.
2. N. Lazaris, Interview.
3. N. Lazaris, Interview.
4. N. Lazaris, Interview.
5. N. Lazaris, Interview.
6. S. Turer, Interviewee, [Interview], 2 Feb 2017.
7. S. Turer, Interview.
8. S. Turer, Interview.
9. S. Turer, Interview.
10. S. Turer, Interview.
11. J. DeRupo, Interviewee, [Interview], 20 Dec 2016.
12. AFP, *Taipei Times*, 22 August 2016, [Online], Available: http://www.taipei times.com/News/biz/archives/2016/08/22/2003653590. [Accessed March 2017].

13. Corporate site [Online], Available: http://www.nestle.com/media/newsand-features/nescafe-75-years.
14. Corporate site [Online], Available: http://www.nestleusa.com/media/nespresso-history-eric-favre-coffee-vacation, [Accessed 15 March 2017].
15. *WIPO*, Sept 2010, [Online], Available: http://www.wipo.int/wipo_magazine /en/2010/05/article_0007.html, [Accessed March 2017].
16. http://www.mars.com/global/about-us/history.
17. K. Noonan, Mars Drinks, Global Corporate Affairs, 9 March 2017.
18. MARS Drinks, 2017, [Online], Available: http://us.myflavia.com/family /index.jsp?categoryId=3414902, [Accessed Feb 2017].
19. Novascientia, 3 Nov 2015, [Online], Available: https://www.novascientia.net /articles/161/Nespresso—A-brand-full-of-Innovation—Patents-and-Lawsuits, [Accessed: Feb 2017].
20. *Global Coffee Report* 17 March 2015, [Online], Available: http://gcrmag .com/news/article/winecombr-purchases-monodor-and-mocoffee [Accessed Feb 2017].

Chapter 5—The K-Cup, an Industry Standard

1. Investopedia, 2017, [Online], Available: http://www.investopedia.com/terms /r/razor-razorblademodel.asp, [Accessed Feb 2017].
2. *USA Today*, 18 Dec 2016, [Online], Available: http://www.usatoday.com/ story/tech/news/2016/12/18/not-quite-keurig-beer-picobrew-brings-craft-beer-brewing-home/95462614/, [Accessed Feb 2017].
3. *Grubstreet*, Nov. 2016, [Online], Available: http://www.grubstreet.com/2016 /11/the-chip-promises-to-be-the-keurig-of-cookies.html, [Accessed Feb 2017].
4. Real Simple, March 2017, [Online], Available: https://www.realsimple.com/ food-recipes/somabar-robotic-bartender-cocktail-machine, [Accessed Feb 2017].
5. M. Haggerty, Interviewee, [Interview], 23 March 2017.
6. R. Sweeney, Interviewee, [Interview], 20 Jan 2017.
7. R. Sweeney, Interviewee.
8. J. Hovis, Interviewee, [Interview], 10 Feb 2017.
9. R. Beaulieu, Interviewee, [Interview], 13 March 2017.
10. R. Beaulieu, Interview.
11. J. Trucano, Interviewee, [Interview], 7 Feb 2017.
12. J. Trucano, Interview.
13. J. Trucano, Interview.

Chapter 6—The Nascent Keurig and the K-Cup

1. N. Lazaris, Interview.
2. N. Lazaris, Interview.
3. N. Lazaris, Interview.
4. N. Lazaris, Interview.
5. N. Lazaris, Interview.
6. N. Lazaris, Interview.
7. MARS Drinks, 2017.
8. N. Lazaris, Interview.
9. N. Lazaris, Interview.
10. N. Lazaris, Interview.
11. N. Lazaris, Interview.
12. N. Lazaris, Interview.
13. N. Lazaris, Interview.
14. Wikipedia [Online] Available: https://en.wikipedia.org/wiki/Senseo, [Accessed Feb 2017].
15. J. Nolan, *AP News Archive*, 17 Feb 2004, [Online], Available: www.apnews archive.com/2004/P-G-Enters-Single-Serving-Coffee-Brewing/id-6c6eb6d-4d6703547566e7a187c5d2e5d, [Accessed Feb 2017].
16. *Enquirer* (Cincinnati), 17 Feb 2004, [Online], Available: http://www.enquirer.com/editions/2004/02/17/biz_biz1coffee.html, [Accessed Feb 2017].
17. N. Lazaris, Interview.
18. N. Lazaris, Interview.
19. N. Lazaris, Interview.
20. N. Lazaris, Interview.
21. *Wall Street Journal*, 7 December 2017, [Online], Available: http://blogs.wsj.com/moneybeat/2015/12/07/meet-jab-the-new-owners-of-keurig-green-mountain/, [Accessed March 2017].
22. *Financial Times,* 8 Dec 2015 [Online], Available: https://www.ft.com/content/2dfdb02e-9dc6-11e5-8ce1-f6219b685d74, [Accessed March 2017].

Chapter 7—K-Cup, Etcetera

1. N. Lazaris, Interview.
2. N. Lazaris, Interview.
3. N. Lazaris, Interview.
4. S. Van Winkle, Interviewee, [Interview], 20 Jan 2017.
5. S. Van Winkle, Interview.

6. S. Van Winkle, Interview.
7. S. Van Winkle, Interview.
8. S. Van Winkle, Interview.
9. S. Van Winkle, Interview.
10. S. Van Winkle, Interview.
11. S. Van Winkle, Interview.
12. S. Van Winkle, Interview.
13. S. Van Winkle, Interview.
14. S. Van Winkle, Interview.
15. S. Van Winkle, Interview.
16. Bloomberg, 28 June 2016, [Online], Available: https://www.bloomberg.com/ news/articles/2016-06-28/nestle-leans-on-nespresso-s-kid-brother-as-coffee-growth-lags, [Accessed March 2017].
17. *PR Newsire*, 1 Oct 2015, [Online], Available: http://www.prnewswire.com /news-releases/nespresso-expands-the-vertuoline—range-with-the-new-evoluo-machine-300152267.html, [Accessed March 2017].
18. Nestle-Nespresso site, [Online], Available: https://www.nestle-nespresso.com/ newsandfeatures/nespresso-sets-to-revolutionise-north-american-coffee-market, [Accessed March 2017].
19. *Financial Times*, 16 May 2014, [Online], Available: https://www.ft.com/content /10849b64-dd08-11e3-b73c-00144feabdc0, [Accessed March 2017].
20. *Reuters*, 17 Aug 2016, [Online], Available: http://www.reuters.com/article /nestle-coffee-idUSL1N1AX0N0, [Accessed March 2017].
21. *Financial Times*, 16 May 2014, [Online], Available: https://www.ft.com /content/10849b64-dd08-11e3-b73c-00144feabdc0, [Accessed March 2017].
22. S. Virani, *Ivey Business Review*, 24 March 2016, [Online], Available: http: //iveybusinessreview.ca/blogs/sviranihba2017/2016/03/24/nespresso-stirring-pod-2/, [Accessed: March 2017].
23. Bloomberg, 28 June 2016.

Chapter 8—Turf Wars: Keep Your Pod Out of My Brewer

1. SEC, [Online], Available: https://www.sec.gov/Archives/edgar/data/909954 /000090995407000002/release_patent.htm, [Accessed Feb 2017].
2. Consumer Goods Technology, 24 Oct 2008, [Online], https://consumergoods .com/kraft-and-green-mountain-coffee-agree-settle, [Accessed: Feb 2017].
3. Protecting Designs, 11 Nov 2011, [Online], Available: http://www.protecting designs.com/keurig-sues-rogers-family-co-over-single-serve-coffee-container-design, [Accessed Feb 2017].

4. *Reuters*, 22 Aug 2014, [Online], Available: http://www.reuters.com/article /us-treehouse-pods-ruling-idUSKBN0GM21Z20140822, [Accessed: Feb 2017].

5. US Courts site, [Online], Available: http://media.ca7.uscourts.gov/cgi-bin /rssExec.pl?Submit=Display&Path=Y2014/D08-22/C:13-3843:J: Wood:aut:T:fnOp:N:1404733:S:0, [Accessed: Feb. 2017].

6. Top Class Actions, [Online], Available: https://topclassactions.com/lawsuit-settlements/lawsuit-news/1313-keurig-k-cup-sturm-foods-class-action-lawsuit/, [Accessed: Feb 2017].

7. Class Dismissed, 10 Nov 2015, [Online], Available: http://classdismissed .mofo.com/food-misbranding/consumers-win-class-certification-in-sturm-foods-grove-square-coffee-pod-suit/, [Accessed: Feb 2017].

8. Gilman Law, LLP, [Online], Available: http://www.gilmanlawllp.com/ consumer-protection/kraft-starbucks-false-advertising-lawsuit-tassimo-coffee-brewing-system/, Accessed: Feb 2017].

9. PR Web, 23 Feb 2012, [Online], Available: http://www.prweb.com/releases /2012/2/prweb9220572.htm, [Accessed: Feb 2017].

10. Top Class Actions, [Online], Available: https://topclassactions.com/lawsuit-settlements/lawsuit-news/26946-tassimo-starbucks-class-action-lawsuit-denied-certification/, [Accessed: Feb 2017].

11. Top Class Actions, [Online], Available: https://topclassactions.com/lawsuit-settlements/lawsuit-news/335672-6th-circuit-affirms-dismissal-tassimo-starbucks-class-action/, [Accessed: Feb 2017].

12. Lawyers.Com, [Online], Available: http://class-actions.lawyers.com/class-action-basics.html, [Accessed: Feb 2017].

13. Truth in Advertising, May 2015, [Online], Available: https://www.truthin advertising.org/wp-content/uploads/2014/05/Montgomery-v-Kraft-appellate-court-decision.pdf, [Accessed: Feb 2017].

14. Law 360, 24 May 2013, [Online], Available: https://www.law360.com /articles/445038/rival-s-coffee-pods-don-t-infringe-keurig-patents-judge-says, [Accesses: Feb 2017].

15. *Food Business News*, 12 Feb 2014, [Online], Available: http://www.food businessnews.net/articles/news_home/Business_News/2014/02/TreeHouse _sues_Green_Mountain.aspx?ID={963532FA-6C3A-4C54-9B09-6A8A6CCD25E5}, [Accessed: Feb 2017].

16. *PR Newswire*, 11 Feb 2014, [Online], Available: http://www.prnewswire.com /news-releases/treehouse-foods-sues-green-mountain-coffee-and-keurig-for-anticompetitive-conduct-lawsuit-seeks-to-preserve-consumer-choice-and-price-competition-in-k-cup-market-244959221.html, [Accessed: Feb 2017].

17. Document cloud, [Online], Available: https://assets.documentcloud.org /documents/1031250/treehouse-v-greenmountain.pdf, [Accessed Feb. 2017].

18. *PR Newswire*, 13 March 2014, [Online], Available: http://www.prnewswire .com/news-releases/rogers-family-co-files-lawsuit-against-keurig-green-mountain-inc-for-alleged-anti-competitive-single-serve-coffee-market-conduct-that-rogers-believes-has-harmed-consumers-250209461.html, [Accessed: Fen 2017].

19. *PR Newswire*, 13 March 2014.

20. *USA Today*, 22 April 2014, [Online], Available: http://www.usatoday. com/story/news/nation/2014/04/22/lawsuits-claim-k-cup-maker-violates-antitrust-laws/8028197/, [Accessed: Feb 2017].

21. *Burlington Free Press*, 12 April 2014, [Online], Available: http://www.burling tonfreepress.com/story/news/2014/04/12/lawsuits-claim -keurig-green-mountain-violating-antitrust-laws/7612125/, [Accessed March 2017].

22. Lexology, 15 Sept 2014, [Online], Available: http://www.lexology.com/library /detail.aspx?g=e23d72a7-8d8e-4f9f-a5ef-3f2751a932a4, [Accessed: Feb 2017].

23. Novascientia, 3 Nov 2015 [Online].

24 *Republique Francaise Autorite de la Concurrence*, 17 April 2014, [Online], Available: http://www.autoritedelaconcurrence.fr/user/standard.php?id_rub =592&id_article=2343, [Accessed: March 2017].

25. *Wall Street Journal*, 17 April 2014, [Online], Available: https://www.wsj.com /articles/SB10001424052702304626304579507060960147686, [Accessed: March 2017].

26. Scribd.com, [Online], Available: https://www.scribd.com/doc/222741728 /Nespresso-v-HiLine-Coffee, [Accessed: Feb 2017].

27. Law 360, [Online], Available: https://www.law360.com/articles/537186 /nespresso-hits-competitor-with-ip-suit-over-coffee-capsules, [Accessed: Feb 2017].

28. *PR Newswire*, 4 Nov 2013, [Online], Available: http://www.prnewswire.com /news-releases/new-coffee-company-offers-premium-alternative-to-nespresso-capsules-230505911.html, [Accessed: Feb 2017].

29. Rogers Family Company, 2 April 2015, [Online], Available: http://www.rogers familyco.com/index.php/letter-founder-ceo-freedom-clip-customers/, [Accessed: Feb 2017].

30. Rogers Family Company, 24 Nov 2014, [Online], Available: http://www.rogers familyco.com/index.php/revolution-begun-starts-now-fight-keurig/, [Accessed: Feb 2017].

31. Rogers Family Company, 27 April 2015, [Online], Available: http://www .rogersfamilyco.com/index.php/introducing-freedom-ring/, [Accessed: Feb 2017].

32. Industry Week, 19 Jan 2015, [Online], Available: http://www.industryweek. com/intellectual-property/nestle-sued-swiss-company-over-nespresso-patent, [Accessed: Feb 2017].

33. Mondaq, 20 May 2014, [Online], Available: http://www.mondaq.com/ france/x/313330/Trade+Regulation+Practices/Nespresso+Offers+Commitments+To+The+French+Competition+Authority+In+CoffeeCapsule+Probe, [Accessed: Feb 2017].

34. *News.com.au*, 20 Jan 2015, http://www.news.com.au/finance/business /manufacturing/shots-fired-swiss-firm-ethical-coffee-company-fights-nestleover-coffee-capsules/news-story/f60b1d41036a6924c49b6cef5058ac7d, [Accessed: Feb 2017].

35. *News.com.au*, 22 Jan 2016, [Online], Available: http://www.news.com.au /finance/business/media/nespresso-sues-israeli-coffee-company-over-clooneylookalike/news-story/63fcd3cdb9a491d3f64ca471c242869a, [Accessed: Feb 2017].

36. *New York Post*, 21 Jan 2016, [Online], Available: http://nypost.com/2016/01/21 /nespresso-sues-israeli-coffee-company-over-george-clooney-clone/, [Accessed: Feb 2017].

37. *Forbes*, 31 Jan 2016, [Online], Available: https://www.forbes.com/sites /guymartin/2016/01/31/nestle-nespresso-george-clooney-lookalike-lawsuit-israel-espresso-club/#1f05ce32348e, [Accessed: Feb 2017].

Chapter 9—The Single-Serve Environmental Quandary and Some Alternatives

1. J. W. Rogers, Interviewee [Interview], 22 Dec 2016.

2. H. Peterson, "Business Insider," 6 May 2015, [Online], Available: http:// www.businessinsider.com/keurig-20-is-hurting-sales-2015-5, [Accessed Jan 2017].

3. A. Hern, *The Guardian*, 11 May 2015, [Online], Available: https://www.the guardian.com/technology/2015/may/11/keurig-takes-steps-towards-abandoningcoffee-pod-drm, [Accessed Jan 2017].

4. J. Dzieza, "The Verge," 5 Feb 2015, [Online], Available: http://www.the verge.com/2015/2/5/7986327/keurigs-attempt-to-drm-its-coffee-cups-totallybackfired, [Accessed Jan 2017].

5. C. Howard, "Clark," 25 Oct 2016, [Online], Available: http://www.clark.com /how-hack-your-keurig-20, [Accessed Jan 2017].

6. Green Day, Interviewee, [Email Interview], 13 Feb 2017.

7. Keurig, March 2017, [Online], Available: http://www.keuriggreenmountain
   .com/en/Sustainability/Overview.aspx, [Accessed March 2017].
8. Kill the KCup, 2016, [Online], Available: https://www.killthekcup.org,
   [Accessed Feb 2017].
9. "Keurig," March 2017, [Online], Available: http://www.keurig.com/recyclable,
   [Accessed March 2017].
10. Keurig, March 2017, [Online], Available: http://www.keuriggreenmountain
    .com/en/Sustainability/SustainableProducts/RecyclablePods.aspx, [Accessed:
    March 2017].
11. Keurig, March 2017, [Online], Available: http://www.keuriggreenmountain
    .com/~/media/Sustainability/PDF/ReportsDisclosures/KeurigSustainability
    Brochure_2015.ashx, [Accessed: Feb 2017].
12. Keurig, March 2017, [Online], Available: http://www.keuriggreenmountain.
    com/~/media/Files/PDF/Media%20Library/Fact%20Sheets/Recyclable%20
    K-Cup%20Fact%20Sheet_June%202016.ashx. [Accessed: March 2017].
13. Mintel, Ltd. Mintel.com, "Global Food & Drink Trends 2017, Mintel,"
    Mintel Food & Drink, 2017.

Chapter 10—Giving Back

1. David Steingard, Interviewee, [Interview], 8 March 2017.
2. Green Day, Interview.
3. Oakland Coffee, Feb 2017, [Online], Available: https://oaklandcoffee.com
   /fueled-by-love/, [Accessed: Feb 2017].
4. Crescendos Alliance, Feb 2017, [Online], Available: http://crescendosalliance
   .com/, [Accessed: Feb 2017].
5. Green Day, Interview.
6. Rogers Family, Feb 2017, [Online], Available: http://www.rogersfamilyco
   .com/index.php/category/on-the-farm/, [Accessed: Feb 2017].
7. J. W. Roger, Interview.

Chapter 11—Coffee and Health

1. *Prevention*, 6 May 2014, [Online], Available: http://www.prevention.com
   /health/infographic-health-benefits-coffee, [Accessed Feb 2017].
2. S. Simon, American Cancer Society, 14 Sept 2016, [Online], Available: https:
   //www.cancer.org/latest-news/can-coffee-lower-cancer-risk.html, [Accessed
   Jan 2017].

3. Harvard Health Publishing, Aug 2004, [Online], Available: http://www .health.harvard.edu/press_releases/coffee_health_risk, [Accessed Jan 2017].

4. Dr. Cornelis, Interviewee, [Interview], 3 Feb 2017.

5. A. Powell, *Harvard Gazette*, 7 Oct 2014, [Online], Available: http://news .harvard.edu/gazette/story/2014/10/java-in-the-genes/.

6. C. Moore, Parkinson's News Today, 2 Oct 2016, [Online], Available: https: //parkinsonsnewstoday.com/2015/10/02/coffee-drinking-lowers-risk-parkin-sons-type-2-diabetes-five-cancers-harvard-researchers/, [Accessed Jan 2017].

7. B. Wu, *Medical News Today*, 17 June 2016, [Online], Available: http: //www.medicalnewstoday.com/articles/311180.php, [Accessed Feb 2017].

8. A. Curry, *Diabetes Forecast*, July 2016, [Online], Available: http://www .diabetesforecast.org/2016/jul-aug/can-a-cup-of-coffee-prevent. html?referrer=http://google.diabetes.org/search?site=Diabetes&client=diabe-tes&entqr=3&oe=ISO-8859-1&ie=ISO-8859-1&ud=1&proxystylesheet=di-abetes&output=xml_no_dtd&proxyreload=1&q=coff, [Accessed Jan 2017].

9. Shilpa N. Bhupathiraju, et al., "Diabetologia," 21 March 2014, [Online], Available: https://cdn1.sph.harvard.edu/wp-content/uploads/sites/21/2014/04 /Changes-in-coffee-intake-and-subsequent-risk-of-type-2-diabetes_-Bhupathira .pdf, [Accessed Jan 2017].

10. World Atlas, 2017, [Online], Available: http://www.worldatlas.com/articles /top-10-coffee-consuming-nations.html, [Accessed Jan 2017].

11. Reference.com, Jan 2017, [Online], Available: https://www.reference.com /science/chlorogenic-acid-8a046d69050a3064, [Accessed Jan 2017].

12. Reference.com, Jan 2017.

13. Sanjiv Chopra, MD, with David Fisher, *The Big 5: Five Sample Things You Can Do to Live a Longer, Healthier Life*, (New York, 2016).

14. Sanjiv Chopra, MD, Interviewee, [Interview], 14 Feb 2017.

15. Neal D. Freedman et al., *The New England Journal of Medicine*, 17 May 2012, [Online], Available: http://www.nejm.org/doi/full/10.1056/NEJMoa1112010 #t=article, [Accessed Feb 2017].

16. Dr. Cornelis, Interview.

17. E. Sage, "The Specialty Coffee Chronicle," 11 July 2014, [Online], Available: http://scaa.org/chronicle/2014/07/11/coffee-roasting-chemistry-chlorogenic-acids/, [Accessed Jan 2017].

18. S. Eckelkamp, *Fox News*, 25 April 2016, [Online], Available: http://www .foxnews.com/health/2016/04/25/8-ways-youre-ruining-health-perks-your-coffee.html, [Accessed Jan 2017].

19. C. Kotyczka et al., US National Library of Medicine National Institutes of Health, October 2011, [Online], Available: https://www.ncbi.nlm.nih.gov /pubmed/21809439?report=abstract, [Accessed February 2017].

20. Sanjiv Chopra, Interview.
21. Nobel Prize site, [Online], Available: https://www.nobelprize.org/nobel_prizes/medicine/laureates/2009/press.html, [Accessed March 2017].
22. Sanjiv Chopra with David Fisher, *The Big* 5.
23. Sanjiv Chopra, Interview.
24. WebMD, 2017, [Online], Available: http://www.webmd.com/migraines-headaches/guide/triggers-caffeine#1, [Accessed Jan 2017].
25. WebMD, 2017.
26. A. Ascherio et al., NCBI, July 2001, [Online], Available: https://www.ncbi.nlm.nih.gov/pubmed/11456310, [Accessed Jan 2017].
27. Sanjiv Chopra with David Fisher, *The Big* 5.
28. HSPH, Jan 2017, [Online], Available: https://www.hsph.harvard.edu/news/multimedia-article/benefits/, [Accessed Jan 2017].
29. Ming Ding et al., *Circulation*, 7 Nov 2013, [Online], Available: http://circ.aha-journals.org/content/early/2013/11/07/CIRCULATIONAHA.113.005925, [Accessed Jan 2017].
30. HSPH, Jan 2017, [Online], Available: https://www.hsph.harvard.edu/news/hsph-in-the-news/coffee-depression-women-ascherio-lucas/, [Accessed Jan 2017].
31. Tori Rodriguez, *Psychiatry Advisor*, 25 March 2016, [Online], Available: http://www.psychiatryadvisor.com/mood-disorders/does-coffee-and-caffeine-lower-risk-of-depression/article/485602/, [Accessed Jan 2017].
32. J. Steenhuysen, *Reuters*, 27 Sept 2011, [Online], Available: http://www.reuters.com/article/us-coffee-depression-idUSTRE78Q3GK20110927, [Accessed Jan 2017].
33. Science Daily, 7 March 2017, [Online], Available: https://www.sciencedaily.com/releases/2017/03/170307130903.htm, [Accessed 8 March 2017].
34. "Medicines in My Home: Caffeine and Your Body," 2007, [Online], Available: https://www.fda.gov/downloads/UCM200805.pdf, [Accessed Jan 2017].
35. Sanjiv Chopra with David Fisher, *The Big* 5.
36. WebMD, 2017.

Chapter 12—Does Single Serve Fuel Too Much Separateness?

1. Ben Waber et al., *Harvard Business Review*, Oct 2014, [Online], Available: https://hbr.org/2014/10/workspaces-that-move-people, [Accessed Jan 2017].
2. A. Pentland, *Harvard Business Review*, "The New Science of Building Great Teams," April 2012, [Online], Available: https://hbr.org/2012/04/the-new-science-of-building-great-teams, [Accessed Feb 2017].

3. Ben Waber et al., *Harvard Business Review.*

4. Ben Waber et al., *Harvard Business Review.*

5. Ben Waber et al., *Harvard Business Review.*

6. NCA 2016 Single Cup Brewing.

7. H. Ward, "The Specialty Coffee Chronicle," 6 Dec 2016, [Online], Available: http://scaa.org/chronicle/2016/12/06/specialty-coffee-shops-market-size-in-the-u-s/, [Accessed March 2017].

8. H. Ward, "The Specialty Coffee Chronicle."

9. H. Gunn, "The Best of Pennsyvania," March 2017, [Online], Available: https://bestthingspa.com/coffee-shops-cafes/, [Accessed March 2017].

10. C. Riehl McMillin, Interviewee, 2017.

11. R. Nowland, Interviewee [Email Interview], 20 March 2017.

Chapter 13—Just What is Single Serve Anyway?

1. Coffee Quality Institute, 2017, [Online], Available: http://www.coffeeinstitute.org/our-work/q-coffee-system/what-is-a-q-grader/, [Accessed March 2017].

2. M. Alves, Interview.

3. A. Atkinson, Interviewee, [Interview], 24 Feb 2017.

4. M. Stark, "The Specialty Coffee Chronicle," Feb 2012, [Online], Available: http://scaa.org/chronicle/2012/02/14/direct-trade-the-questions-answers/, [Accessed March 2017].

5. A. Feldman, Lexicon of Food, 20 May 2015, [Online], Available: https://www.lexiconoffood.com/definition/definition-direct-trade, [Accessed Feb 2017].

6. A. Atkinson, Interview.

7. La Colombe, [Online], Available: https://www.lacolombe.com/, [Accesses March 2017].

8. Mintel, March 2017, [Online], Available: http://www.mintel.com/press-centre/food-and-drink/coffee-brews-up-success-in-asia, [Accessed March 2017].

9. Mintel, March 2017.

10. Starbucks, March 2017, [Online], Available: http://store.starbucks.com/coffee/starbucks-via-instant-coffee/, [Accessed March 2017].

11. Matthew Barry and Virginia Lee, *Global Trends in Instant Coffee*, Euromonitor International, 2016, www.euromonitor.com.

12. Mintel, March 2017.

13. Mintel, March 2017.

Chapter 14—What's Next for Coffee for One?

1. Business Insider, 20 Oct 2015, [Online], Available: http://www.businessinsider.com/10-technology-related-things-back-to-the-future-ii-got-right-about-2015-2015-10/#mobile-credit-card-readers-6, [Accessed: March 2017].
2. James Cave, *Huffington Post*, 20 Jan 2016, [Online], Available: http://www.huffingtonpost.com/entry/gucci-fall-2016-mens-milan_us_569e664be4b-0cd99679b6436, [Accessed: March 2017].
3. Mintel, "Global Food & Drink Trends."
4. NootroBox, [Online], Available: https://nootrobox.com/go-cubes, [Accessed: Feb 2017].
5. J. Traeger, Traeger Communications, Interviewee [Email Interview], [17 Feb 2017].
6. Soylent, Jan 2017, [Online], Available: https://www.soylent.com/product/cafe/, [Accessed Jan 2017].
7. Goat Story, Feb 2017, [Online], Available: http://www.goat-story.com/, [Accessed Feb 2017].
8. IndieGoGo, Jan 2017, [Online], Available: https://www.indiegogo.com/projects/the-barisieur-coffee-design#/, [Accessed Jan 2017].
9. The Barisieur, Jan 2017, [Online], Available: http://www.barisieur.com/, [Accessed Jan 2017].
10. Cafe X, Feb 2017, [Online], Available: https://cafexapp.com/, [Accessed Feb 2017].
11. M. Petrova, *PC World*, 3 Feb 2017, [Online], Available: http://www.pcworld.com/article/3165332/techology-business/this-robotic-barista-never-needs-a-coffee-break.html?google_editors_picks=true, [Accessed Feb 2017].
12. Spinn, [Online], Available: https://www.spinn.com/, [Accessed: March 2017].
13. Bunn, [Online], Available: https://homecatalog.bunn.com/category/Home-Catalog-US/BREWERS/SINGLE-CUP, [Accessed: March 2017].

Bibliography

"Ad Man Cautions Coffee Men to Modernize Coffee's Image; Sees Coffee as Drink of the '80s." *World Coffee & Tea*. 1981: 76-78.

AFP. *Taipei Times*. August 22, 2016. http://www.taipeitimes.com/News /biz/archives/2016/08/22/2003653590. (accessed March 2017).

Ascherio A., Zhang S. M., Hernán M. A., Kawachi I., Colditz G. A., Speizer F. E., Willett W. C. NCBI. July 2001. https://www.ncbi.nlm.nih.gov /pubmed/11456310. (accessed Jan 2017).

Barry, Matthew and Virginia Lee. *Global Trends in Instant Coffee*. Market Research, Euromonitor International. 2016.

"Bring Back Jolt." Sept 4, 2017. https://www.facebook.com/pg/bringbackjolt /about/?ref=page_internal. (accessed Sept 4, 2017).

Bhupathiraju, Shilpa N, An Pan, JoAnn E. Manson, Walter C. Willett, Rob M. van Dam, Frank B. Hu. "Diabetologia." March 21, 2014. https://cdn1.sph.harvard.edu/wp-content/uploads/sites/21/2014/04/ Changes-in-coffee-intake-and-subsequent-risk-of-type-2-diabetes _Bhupathira.pdf. (accessed Jan 2017).

Cafe Cola. Sept 4, 2017. http://cafecola.com/. (accessed Sept 4, 2017).

Cafe X. Feb 2017. https://cafexapp.com/. (accessed Feb 2017).

Cleveland Clinic. 2017. http://my.clevelandclinic.org/health/articles/caffeine-and-headache. (accessed Jan 2017).

Coffee & Cocoa International. "Giants Clash in Specialty Brands War." *Coffee and Cocoa International* 13(5):9. *C&CI*. 1986.

"Coffee Lab Intl." Feb 2017. http://www.coffeelab.com/quality-assurance-coffee-testing.html. (accessed Feb 2017).

Coffee Quality Institute. 2017. http://www.coffeeinstitute.org/our-work /q-coffee-system/what-is-a-q-grader/. (accessed March 2017).

"Coffee Research." n.d. http://www.coffeeresearch.org/market/frosthistory .htm. (accessed Jan 2017).

Cornelis, Dr. Interview by K. J. Fallon. (Feb 3, 2017).

"Cupping Protocols." March 2017. http://www.scaa.org/?page=resources&d =cupping-protocols. (accessed March 2017).

Curry, Andrew. *Diabetes Forecast.* July 2016. http://www.diabetesforecast. org/2016/jul-aug/can-a-cup-of-coffee-prevent.html?referrer=http://google .diabetes.org/search?site=Diabetes&client=diabetes&entqr=3&oe=ISO-8859-1&ie=ISO-8859-1&ud=1&proxystylesheet=diabetes&output=xml_ no_dtd&proxyreload=1&q=coff. (accessed Jan 2017).

Danovich, Tove. "Why Big Soda Is Still Fighting for a Place at the Breakfast Table." Feb 15, 2016. http://www.eater.com/2016/2/15/10976654 /breakfast-soda-drinking-trend. (accessed Feb 2007).

Ding, Ming, Shilpa N. Bhupathiraju, Ambika Satija, Rob M. van Dam, Frank B. Hu. *Circulation.* Nov 7, 2013. http://circ.ahajournals.org/content/early/2013/11/07/CIRCULATIONAHA.113.005925. (accessed Jan 2017).

Dzieza, Josh. "The Verge." Feb 5, 2015. http://www.theverge.com/2015 /2/5/7986327/keurigs-attempt-to-drm-its-coffee-cups-totally-backfired. (accessed Jan 2017).

Eckelkamp, Stephanie. *Fox News.* April 25, 2016. http://www.foxnews .com/health/2016/04/25/8-ways-youre-ruining-health-perks-yourcoffee.html. (accessed Jan 2017).

"Euromonitor, a market research provider." September 2017. www.euromonitor.com. (accessed September 13, 2017).

Feldman, Andrew. Lexicon of Food. May 20, 2015. https://www.lexiconoffood.com/definition/definition-direct-trade. (accessed Feb 2017).

Freedman, Neal D., Ph.D., Yikyung Park, Sc.D., Christian C. Abnet, Ph.D., Albert R. Hollenbeck, Ph.D., and Rashmi Sinha, Ph.D. *The*

New England Journal of Medicine. May 17, 2012. http://www.nejm.org /doi/full/10.1056/NEJMoa1112010#t=article. (accessed Feb 2017).

Goat Story. Feb 2017. http://www.goat-story.com/. (accessed Feb 2017).

Gunn, Hilary. "The Best of Pennsyvania." March 2017. https://bestthing-spa.com/coffee-shops-cafes/. (accessed March 2017).

Haley, Jean Buzby and Stephen. "Coffee Consumption over the Last Century." June 1, 2007. https://www.ers.usda.gov/amber-waves/2007/june/ coffee-consumption-over-the-last-century/. (accessed March 2017).

"Harvard Health Publishing." Aug 2004. http://www.health.harvard.edu /press_releases/coffee_health_risk. (accessed Jan 2017).

Hern, Alex. *The Guardian.* May 11, 2015. https://www.theguardian.com /technology/2015/may/11/keurig-takes-steps-towards-abandoning -coffee-pod-drm. (accessed Jan 2017).

History Is Served. "Beer for Breakfast." March 2017. http://recipes.history .org/2014/09/beer-for-breakfast/. (accessed March 2017).

"History of Coffee." n.d. http://www.ethiopianspecialtycoffee.com/his-tory.htm. (accessed Jan 2017).

"History of the Coffeemaker." Feb 2017. http://www.coffee.org/History-of-the-Coffee-Maker. (accessed Feb 2017).

Howard, Clark. "Clark." Oct 25, 2016. http://www.clark.com/how-hack-your-keurig-20. (accessed Jan 2017).

HSPH. Jan 2017. https://www.hsph.harvard.edu/news/multimedia-article /benefits/. (accessed Jan 2017).

HSPH. Jan 2017. https://www.hsph.harvard.edu/news/hsph-in-the-news /coffee-depression-women-ascherio-lucas/. (accessed Jan 2017).

IndieGoGo. Jan 2017. https://www.indiegogo.com/projects/the-barisieur-coffee-design#/. (accessed Jan 2017).

"International Coffee Organization." 2017. http://www.ico.org/icohistory_e. asp. (accessed Jan 2017).

Investopedia. 2017. http://www.investopedia.com/terms/r/razor-razorblade model.asp. (accessed Feb 2017).

Keurig. March 2017. http://www.keuriggreenmountain.com/en/Sustainability/Overview.aspx. (accessed March 2017).

Keurig. March 2017. http://www.keurig.com/recyclable. (accessed March 2017).

Keurig Green Mountain Shares Progress on Sustainability Commitments. June 13, 2017. http://news.keuriggreenmountain.com/press-release/sustainability/keurig-green-mountain-shares-progress-sustainability-commitments. (accessed September 11, 2017).

Kill the KCup. 2016. https://www.killthekcup.org. (accessed Feb 2017).

Kotyczka C., U. Boettler, R. Lang, H. Stiebitz, G. Bytof, I. Lantz, T. Hofmann, D. Marko, V. Somoza. US National Library of Medicine National Institutes of Health. October 2011. https://www.ncbi.nlm.nih.gov/pubmed/21809439?report=abstract. (accessed February 2017).

LA Times from *The Washington Post.* "Alternative Caffeine Fix: Coke if Popping Up on the Morning Menu." Dec 2, 1987. http://articles.latimes.com/1987-12-02/business/fi-17237_1_coke. (accessed Jan 2017).

Lazaris, Nick. Interview by K. J. Fallon. (Jan 17, 2017).

Lillie, Barry. "Italian Coffee Culture." *Italy Magazine.* Nov 4, 2013. http://www.italymagazine.com/featured-story/italian-coffee-culture. (accessed March 2017).

"LLoyds of London Corporate History." March 2017. https://www.lloyds.com/lloyds/about-us/history/corporate-history. (accessed Feb 2017).

MARS Drinks. 2017. http://us.myflavia.com/family/index.jsp?categoryId=3414902. (accessed Feb 2017).

Marshall, Colin. *The Guardian.* May 14, 2015. https://www.theguardian.com/cities/2015/may/14/the-first-starbucks-coffee-shop-seattle-a-history-of-cities-in-50-buildings-day-36. (accessed Jan 2017).

Massimo Zanetti. n.d. https://www.mzb-usa.com/. (accessed March 1, 2017).

"Medicines in My Home: Caffeine and Your Body." 2007. https://www.fda.gov/downloads/UCM200805.pdf. (accessed Jan 2017).

Mintel. March 2017. http://www.mintel.com/press-centre/food-and-drink /coffee-brews-up-success-in-asia. (accessed March 2017).

Mintel, Ltd, Mintel.com. "Global Food & Drink Trends 2017, Mintel." Marketing Report. Mintel Food & Drink. 2017.

Moore, Charles. Parkinson's News Today. Oct 2, 2016. https://parkinsons newstoday.com/2015/10/02/coffee-drinking-lowers-risk-parkin-sons-type-2-diabetes-five-cancers-harvard-researchers/. (accessed Jan 2017).

National Coffee Association. *National Coffee Drinking Trends 2017.* National Coffee Association New York: The National Coffee Associa-tion of USA, Inc., 2017.

National Coffee Association USA. February 2017. http://www.ncausa.org /About-Coffee/History-of-Coffee (accessed February 2017).

National Coffee Association USA. "Coffee Roast Guide." March 2017. http:// www.ncausa.org/About-Coffee/Coffee-Roasts-Guide (accessed March 2017).

National Coffee Assocation. *NCA 2016 Single Cup Brewing, Changing Behaviors and Attitudes.* The NCA Market Research Series. New York: The National Coffee Association of USA, Inc., 2017.

National Coffee Association, "What is Coffee?" 2017. http://www.ncausa. org/About-Coffee/What-is-Coffee (accessed Sept 5, 2017).

National Coffee Association, "10 Steps from Seed to Cup," March 2017. http://www.ncausa.org/About-Coffee/10-Steps-from-Seed-to-Cup. (accessed March 2017).

Nolan, John. *AP News Archive.* Feb 17, 2004. www.apnewsarchive.com /2004/P-G-Enters-Single-Serving-Coffee-Brewing/id-6c6eb6d-4d6703547566e7a187c5d2e5d. (accessed Feb 2017).

Obias, Rudie. "Mental Floss." March 2017. http://mentalfloss.com/article /66433/12-discontinued-products-coca-cola-and-pepsi (accessed March 2017).

Pacific Bag, Inc. n.d. "One-Way Degassing Valve, What Is it?" March 2017. https//www.pacificbag.com/blog/2015/7/8/one-way-degassing-valve-what-is-it (accessed March 1, 2017).

Pacific Bag, Inc. "A History of Coffee Bags." March 2017. https://www
.pacificbag.com/blog/2015/7/8/a-history-of-coffee-bags. (accessed March
2017).

———. "One-Way Degassing Valve, What Is it?" March 2017. https://www
.pacificbag.com/blog/2015/7/8/one-way-degassing-valve-what-is-it.
(accessed March 2017).

Pentland, Alex "Sandy." *Harvard Business Review,* "The New Science of
Building Great Teams." April 2012. https://hbr.org/2012/04/the-new-
science-of-building-great-teams. (accessed Feb 2017).

Peterson, Hayley. "Business Insider." May 6, 2015. http://www.businessin-
sider.com/keurig-20-is-hurting-sales-2015-5. (accessed Jan 2017).

Petrova, Magdalena. *PC World.* Feb 3, 2017. http://www.pcworld.com
/article/3165332/techology-business/this-robotic-barista-never-needs-
a-coffee-break.html?google_editors_picks=true. (accessed Feb 2017).

Powell, Alvin. *Harvard Gazette.* Oct 7, 2014. http://news.harvard.edu
/gazette/story/2014/10/java-in-the-genes/.

———. *Harvard Gazette.* September 28, 2015. http://news.harvard.edu
/gazette/story/2015/09/how-coffee-loves-us-back/. (accessed February
2017).

Prevention. May 6, 2014. http://www.prevention.com/health/infographic
-health-benefits-coffee. (accessed Feb 2017).

"Reference.com." Jan 2017. https://www.reference.com/science/chlorogenic-
acid-8a046d69050a3064. (accessed Jan 2017).

Riehl McMillin, Catherine. Interview by K. J. Fallon. (2017).

Rodriquez, Tori, MA, LPC. *Psychiatry Advisor.* March 25, 2016. http://
www.psychiatryadvisor.com/mood-disorders/does-coffee-and-caf-
feine-lower-risk-of-depression/article/485602/. (accessed Jan 2017).

Rogers, John W. Interview by K. J. Fallon. *VP* (Dec 22, 2016).

Rohter, Larry. *The Washington Post.* June 24, 1979. https://www
.washingtonpost.com/archive/politics/1979/06/24/brazil-awaits-
full-impact-of-early-frost-in-coffee-areas/1476ca19-39ff-493f-b0e2-
fabed0b9295f/?utm_term=.b645e6db95cb. (accessed Jan 2017).

Roseberry, W. "The Rise of Yuppie Coffees and the Reimagination of Class in the United States." *American Anthropologist* 98 (1996): 762–774.

Sage, Emma. "The Specialty Coffee Chronicle." July 11, 2014. http://scaa.org /chronicle/2014/07/11/coffee-roasting-chemistry-chlorogenic-acids/. (accessed Jan 2017).

"Science Daily." March 7, 2017. https://www.sciencedaily.com/releases /2017/03/170307130903.htm. (accessed March 8, 2017).

Selamta. April through June 1996. http://www.selamta.net/Ethiopian%20 Coffee.htm. (accessed February 2017).

Simon, Stacy. American Cancer Society. Sept 14, 2016. https://www.cancer .org/latest-news/can-coffee-lower-cancer-risk.html. (accessed Jan 2017).

Soylent. Jan 2017. https://www.soylent.com/product/coffiest/. (accessed Jan 2017).

Specialty Coffee Association. "Because Great Coffee Doesn't Just Happen." March 2017. http://scaa.org/?page=work. (accessed March 2017).

Starbucks. March 2017. http://store.starbucks.com/coffee/starbucks-via-in-stant-coffee/. (accessed March 2017).

Stark, Mya. "The Specialty Coffee Chronicle." Feb 2012. http://scaa.org/ chronicle/2012/02/14/direct-trade-the-questions-answers/. (accessed March 2017).

Steenhuysen, Julie. *Reuters.* Sept 27, 2011. http://www.reuters.com/article/ us-coffee-depression-idUSTRE78Q3GK20110927. (accessed Jan 2017).

The Barisieur. Jan 2017. http://www.barisieur.com/. (accessed Jan 2017).

"The History of Coffee in Brazil." March 2017. http://www.casabrasilcof-fees.com/learn/history-of-coffee-in-brazil/. (accessed March 2017).

The New York Times. "A Morning Cola Instead of Coffee?" Jan 20, 1988. http://www.nytimes.com/1988/01/20/business/a-morning-cola-instead-of-coffee.html (accessed Jan 2017).

UPI. July 28, 1981. http://www.upi.com/Archives/1981/07/28/Brazil-ian-frost-less-damaging-than-1975/4715365140800/ (accessed Jan 2017).

"U.S. Coffee Drinking Slips after Slight Gain; Young Still not Drinking." *World Coffee & Tea.* 1980: 21–22.

Waber, Ben, Jennifer Magnolfi, Greg Lindsay. *Harvard Busiess Review.* Oct 2014. https://hbr.org/2014/10/workspaces-that-move-people. (accessed Jan 2017).

Ward, Heather. "The Specialty Coffee Chronicle." Dec 6, 2016. http://scaa .org/chronicle/2016/12/06/specialty-coffee-shops-market-size-in-the-u-s/. (accessed March 2017).

WebMD. 2017. http://www.webmd.com/migraines-headaches/guide/trig-gers-caffeine#1. (accessed Jan 2017).

Willett, Andrew, *New York Times,* Jan 17, 2014, https://www.nytimes .com/2014/01/19/nyregion/the-sweet-smell-of-longevity-at-mcnultys .html?_r=0, (accessed Feb 2017).

WIPO. Sept 2010. http://www.wipo.int/wipo_magazine/en/2010/05/article _0007.html. (accessed March 2017).

World Atlas. 2017. http://www.worldatlas.com/articles/top-10-coffee-con-suming-nations.html. (accessed Jan 2017).

Wu, Brian. *Medical News Today.* June 17, 2016. http://www.medicalnews today.com/articles/311180.php. (accessed Feb 2017).

Yoshihara, Nancy. *The Los Angeles Times.* Dec 3, 1986. http://articles.latimes. com/1986-12-03/business/fi-293_1_coffee-market. (accessed March 2017).